Writing

11-14

Connections

Pearson Education
Edinburgh Gate
Harlow
Essex
CM20 2JE

England and Associated Companies throughout the World

ISBN 1405 81358 X

Printed in Spain by Mateu Cromo, S.A. Pinto (Madrid)

First published 2005

The Publisher's policy is to use paper manufactured from sustainable forests

Designed by Jackie Hill 320 Design

Picture research by Louise Edgeworth

Acknowledgements
We are grateful to Brummie Stokes for permission to reproduce an extract from 'Avalanche' from Sherpas and Soldiers: A Taste for Adventure by Brummie Stokes, ISBN 0954 15510 6 (Sales tel: 0044 (0)1432 761398).

We are grateful to the following for permission to reproduce photographs:
A1Pix: pg16(b), pg64, pg93(t), pg96, pg99(t), pg147, pg154; **Alamy:** pg39(Ilya Shadrim), pg42(Worldwide Picture Library), pg48(Popperfoto), pg66-67(ImageState), pg71(Popperfoto), pg72(Steve Morgan), pg103(Simon Weir), pg108(Michael Sugrue), pg115(Ingram Publishing), pg119(Dick Makin), pg129(wherrett.com), pg131(Stockfolio), pg135(Stockfolio), pg139(Popperfoto), pg141(Popperfoto), pg146(Ace Stock Ltd), pg150(Oote Boe), pg153(Arcaid); **Art Directors & TRIP:** pg12(l)(play)(Helene Rogers), pg36(Viesti Collection), pg58-59(Helene Rogers), pg60(Helene Rogers), pg82-83(Picturesque), pg84-85(Alexander Kuznetsov), pg99(b)(Helene Rogers), pg100(Helene Rogers), pg101(Helene Rogers), pg113(Viesti Collection), pg120(Helene Rogers); **Bubbles:** pg10, pg12(r), pg32; **Corbis:** pg24(Anthony John West), pg38(Randy Wells), pg50-51(Dimitri Lundt), pg54(t)(Reuters), pg56(Dimitri Lundt), pg57(Alan Schein Photography), pg73(Firefly Productions), pg81(Patrik Giardino), pg89(Galen Rowell), pg134(Paul Hardy); **Corbis Sygma:** pg91(Kent News & Picture); **Digital Vision:** pg16(t), pg122, pg123(b); **Empics:** pg37(PA), pg40(PA), pg90(t)(PA), pg137(EPA), pg145(PA); **Greg Evans International:** pg11(r), pg13; **ImageState:** pg20-21, pg22, pg23, pg69, pg80, pg148; **Katz:** pg47(Vogelzang Leo/Gamma), pg54(b)(Rodtmann/Laif), pg90(b)(Ian Turner), pg105(Tom Kidd), pg136(De Sota George/Gamma); **Erik Lindkvist (Kingfisher Image Library):** pg143; **NASA:** pg109; **Photofusion:** pg11(l)(Christa Stadtler), pg12(r); **Rex Features:** pg18(Nils Jorgensen), pg26(Sipa Press), pg28(Sipa Press); **Science Photo Library:** pg111(US Geological Survey); **Stone:** pg74(David Young-Wolff), pg123(t)(Matthias Clamer); **Taxi:** pg78(Brooke Slezak), pg124(J P Fruchet), pg126(James Porto), pg128(James Porto); **Travel Ink:** pg93(b)(Chris North), pg94(Chris North); **Tropix:** pg45(Martin Birley), pg97(Roland Birley), pg98(Roland Birley); **John Walmsley:** pg12(c)(computers), pg62.

Cover: ImageState/Alamy

Developing Writing Strategies to Improve Performance

Writing
Connections

11-14

Dr Helen Bulbeck
Bernadette Carroll
Melinda Derry
Michael Duffy
Emma Lee
Glenn Mascord

PEARSON
Longman

Series editor: Bernadette Carroll

Contents

This contents page gives an overview of the units in the book showing the theme and the writing triplet (for example, Persuade, argue, advise) you will explore in each unit. In addition, it lists the writing Assessment Focuses each unit will cover and whether the tasks are longer writing tasks (LW Task) or shorter writing tasks (SW Task).

1 Growing up — Persuade, argue, advise

LW Task 1: Give it a go!
LW Task 2: Have you tried ...?

Using different text types – AF2
Organising the ideas – AF3
Paragraphs and links – AF4
Using different types of sentences – AF5

page 10

2 Emergencies — Inform, explain, describe

SW Task 1: Safety first
SW Task 2: Antarctic emergencies

Interesting texts – AF1
Using different types of sentences – AF5
Range of punctuation – AF6

page 18

3 Healthy eating — Analyse, review, comment

LW Task 1: 'Bad' foods banned!
LW Task 2: Healthy eating for all

Organising the ideas – AF3
Paragraphs and links – AF4
Choice of vocabulary – AF7

page 29

4 Saving animals — Imagine, explore, entertain

SW Task 1: The last tiger
SW Task 2: First sighting

Choice of vocabulary – AF7
Correct spelling – AF8

page 37

5 Sport — Imagine, explore, entertain

LW Task 1: In your dreams
LW Task 2: I didn't think I could do it but ...

Interesting texts – AF1
Organising the ideas – AF3
Range of punctuation – AF6

page 46

6 **The world of work**   **Persuade, argue, advise**

SW Task 1: Selling school subjects   Choice of vocabulary – AF7   page 57
                                            Correct spelling – AF8
SW Task 2: Delivering the right copy

7 **Discoveries**   **Inform, explain, describe**

LW Task 1: The land of the free   Using different types of sentences – AF5   page 64
                                            Choice of vocabulary – AF7
LW Task 2: The last unexplored continent

8 **Rituals**   **Analyse, review, comment**

SW Task 1: How do you celebrate?   Using different text types – AF2   page 73
                                            Range of punctuation – AF6
SW Task 2: Reward review

9 **Violent Earth**   **Imagine, explore, entertain**

LW Task 1: Avalanche!   Interesting texts – AF1   page 82
LW Task 2: Flood alert   Organising the ideas – AF3

10 **Islands**   **Inform, explain, describe**

SW Task 1: The island from the sea   Organising the ideas – AF3   page 92
                                            Paragraphs and links – AF4
SW Task 2: Desert island   Using different types of sentences – AF5
                                            Correct spelling – AF8

11 **Aliens and UFOs**   **Analyse, review, comment**

LW Task 1: Monster in the lake?   Using different text types – AF2   page 102
                                            Organising the ideas – AF3
LW Task 2: Is it worth it?   Paragraphs and links – AF4

Contents

12 Food, glorious food   Persuade, argue, advise

SW Task 1: A little bit of   Interesting texts – AF1   page 112
what you fancy ...   Range of punctuation – AF6
SW Task 2: Cold comfort?

13 New worlds   Inform, explain, describe

LW Task 1: Jungle fever   Interesting texts – AF1   page 122
LW Task 2: Landing on   Organising the ideas – AF3
the red planet   Paragraphs and links – AF4

14 Moving about   Analyse, review, comment

SW Task 1: Getting to   Organising the ideas – AF3   page 129
school   Paragraphs and links – AF4
SW Task 2: Two wheels or feet   Correct spelling – AF8

15 Heroes   Persuade, argue, advise

LW Task 1: We can be   Using different text types – AF2   page 136
heroes   Choice of vocabulary – AF7
LW Task 2: We all need
a hero

16 Places worth saving   Imagine, explore, entertain

SW Task 1: Great buildings!   Interesting texts – AF1   page 147
SW Task 2: A new perspective   Using different types of sentences – AF5

Introduction

Being able to write well depends on your ability to write for different purposes and to meet the needs of specific audiences. To be a successful writer, you need to consider how suitable your words, sentences and paragraphs are for your reader and check that they meet the requirements of the task that you have been given.

Writing Connections 11–14 contains 16 units. Each unit has a different theme and contains two writing tasks. You will learn how to use a wide range of writing strategies to help you to write better responses to these tasks. Let's take a closer look at the structure of a unit.

Title and introduction	After the title of the unit, which tells you the theme, the first thing you'll see is an introduction. The introduction outlines the writing purpose, for example to inform, explain and describe, and skills you will be focusing on in the unit and why they are important for your writing.
Writing strategies	Following this is a list of the writing strategies you will be using during the unit. Look them up on pages 6–7 if you need to remind yourself what they mean.
Pre-writing activity	Next there is a pre-writing activity. This focuses on one of the writing strategies and helps to prepare you for the tasks you are going to attempt in the unit.
Task 1	Then you will see writing Task 1. This gives you a context and format for your writing. It will give you some prompts to help you to think about what and how to write. You will be encouraged to think about the purpose and audience, and what structure and style will be appropriate for your writing.
Model text	A model text follows the task, showing you an example response. This will show you the kinds of features that a successful response to this task could include.
Studying the model text	This will be followed by a sequence of activities to help you explore the features of the model text. As shown in the Contents pages (pages 2–4), the activities are linked to the Assessment Focuses you will meet when you take your national tests. Take note of these because they are a clue about the sort of technique that you are being asked to investigate.
Completing the task	You will then work through each stage of the writing process (**Planning to write**, **Composing** and **Improving**) using a range of writing strategies to help you. In some units you might only complete part of a response to Task 1. Finally you will be asked to **Review** your work, thinking about how successfully you have responded to the task and setting targets for future work.
Task 2	This will be set out in the same way as Task 1. You will need to use the prompts contained in the task to help you to decide what your response will need to include.
Completing the task	As with Task 1, there will be a series of activities to guide you through the writing process. You will practise using the techniques and strategies you have explored earlier in the unit in your own piece of writing.

Writing strategies

Good writers use a range of writing strategies to help them write effectively. The strategies in this list are organised according to the stage in the writing process at which you are most likely to use them. However, some, for example **ask questions** and **see the whole text**, can be used at any stage. Refer to this list as you work through the book to remind you of the strategies you need to use.

Planning

Choose how to plan

- There are different ways of planning your writing, for example: lists, tables, spider diagrams and flowcharts. You need to choose one that is appropriate for the type of writing you are doing. You may find it helpful to refer to the list of planning strategies on pages 8 and 9.

Write for a reader

- Before you start writing, decide what audience you are writing for. What does that reader need you to do in your writing? What will they expect?

Ask questions

- Before you write, think of a few questions linked to the objectives for the task and the features of the piece of writing. Ask yourself questions to generate ideas. During the writing, keep reminding yourself of these questions.
- When you have finished, use these questions as a checklist to make sure you have done what you set out to do.

Composing

See the whole text

- As you are writing, hold in your head an idea of what the finished piece should look like. This is more than the design and layout. In the picture of the piece you should be able to 'see' the main features of how it is organised (how long it is, what sections it has got, how it starts and ends) and the sort of words and sentences it uses. You might be matching it in your head to other examples of the type of writing that you have seen or written yourself.

Use your plan

- Use your plan to help you decide the organisation of your ideas as well as the content.
- As you write, keep looking back at your plan and your notes. You could tick the bits you've done and make a note of any new ideas.

Stick to the objectives

- As you write, remind yourself what you need to do in the piece of writing. You could write key words from the objective on the top of your page or on a card on your desk.
- Check that you are achieving what you set out to do. Use the objective to review your work at the end. Have you been successful?

Use writers' techniques

- Study examples of similar pieces of writing. Identify some techniques those writers have used. Can you use the same techniques in your piece of writing? Keep a list of them or keep a copy of the text beside you as you write.

Rehearse sentences in your head

- Create your sentence in your head (or say it aloud) before you write it down.

Loop back

- Writers re-read their work as they write. This is to check that it makes sense and says what they want it to say. It is also to remind them of what they have said so they can think about what comes next. This is a way of making sure ideas are properly connected so that the reader will be able to follow them. It is like seeing the sentences as a chain of meaning and you are checking that the links are in place.
- After the writing is finished, writers re-read their work. Check that the whole piece makes sense, includes the right information and succeeds in doing what you want it to do.

Think about the effect on the reader

- As you are drafting your writing, decide how you want your reader to feel or respond and how you are going to achieve this. Choose words, sentences and organisational features that will have a particular effect on the reader. Are you going to speak directly to the reader? Are there any surprises for the reader?
- When your writing is complete, imagine you are reading it. What are you thinking? How does it make you feel? Are there any places where you lose interest or need different information? Can you follow what is being said? Do you feel involved in the writing?

Adding

- As you are composing your sentences, in your head, aloud or on paper, think about whether you can add an additional comment, perhaps as an aside. This works in lots of types of writing and allows the voice of the writer or the narrator to be heard. It is also a way of extending your main point so that it is more convincing.

Deleting

- When you improve your first draft, you can often cut out a lot of unnecessary words and sentences. This helps you to make your ideas much more concisely expressed. You might also change or substitute words and sentences as you do this.
- You could work with a partner to review your writing and confirm which sections could be deleted.

Substituting

- In some pieces of writing, you will need to refer to the same thing lots of times. Before you start to write, make a list of different ways to refer to it (e.g. by name, with a synonym, by using a pronoun instead of the noun). When improving your first draft, check that you have used a range of these unless you are deliberately trying not to give information away. You can do the same with the words to open and link your paragraphs and sentences.

Changing

- As you re-read your writing, you will be able to hear where strings of sentences have the same structure and therefore become repetitive. Your writing will have more impact if you vary the structure. This will also allow you to check that you've got very tight links between your ideas and that the points develop logically.
- Sometimes, though, you might want to have lots of sentences with the same structure to create a particular atmosphere.

Planning strategies

It is helpful to be confident about using a range of planning strategies so that you are able to select the one that is most appropriate for each piece of writing you do. Some units in this book will advise you to use a particular planning strategy, but others will ask you to choose how to plan, thinking about the requirements of the task that you have been given. Refer to this list as you work through the book to remind you of some of the different planning strategies you can choose from.

Flow chart

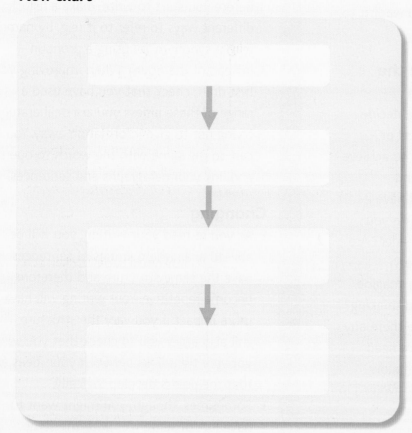

You could use this when you need to:
- Inform about an event
- Explain a process
- Describe a process
- Order events in a story
- Write about something organised in chronological order.

Spider diagram

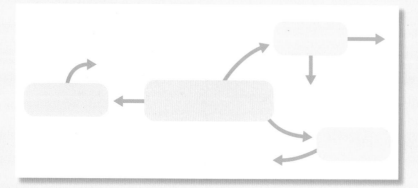

You could use this when you need to:
- Gather ideas
- Describe a scene
- Write something where you need to include lots of ideas and different topics.

Comparison table

	Idea 1	Idea 2
Similarity 1		
Similarity 2		
Similarity 3		

You could use this when you need to:
- Look at two sides of an issue or idea
- Argue a case
- Analyse an issue
- Create contrast in descriptive writing.

Continuum Line

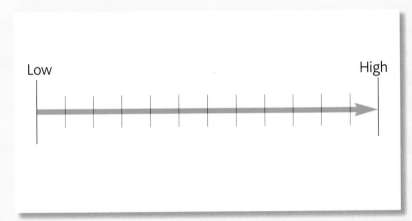

Low   High

You could use this when you need to:
- Think about where you stand on an issue.
- Sequence each point in an argument in order of strength or impact
- Write persuasively
- Consider the importance of your ideas in non-chronological writing.

Fishbone plan

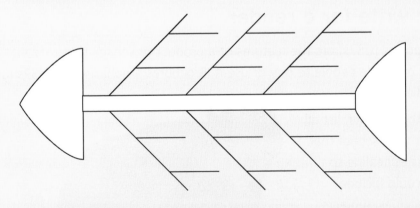

You could use this when you need to:
- Inform a reader
- Explain something to a reader
- Write to argue, using one side for and the other against
- Order persuasive writing
- Order analytical writing.

PEE organiser

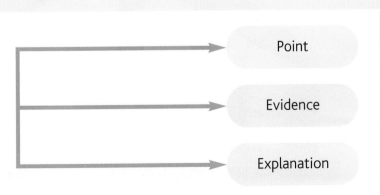

Point

Evidence

Explanation

You could use this when you need to:
- Add to a fishbone plan
- Analyse an issue
- Argue a case
- Write persuasively
- Explain something to a reader.

Growing up

Persuade, argue, advise

When you are writing to persuade, argue and advise, you must be aware of your target audience because the aim is to change the way people think or act in the future. You can find this type of writing in brochures for holidays or activities, which directly address the reader and try to persuade him or her to do or buy something, often by making it sound exciting. Most persuasive writing is structured as a series of points, linked together, which give information and support one particular viewpoint. In this unit you will explore how using different sentence types and lengths can help to persuade the reader. You will also consider the different ways writers can 'speak' to different readers.

Writing strategies

- write for a reader
- use writers' techniques
- think about the effect on the reader
- rehearse sentences in your head
- changing

Pre-writing: write for a reader

1   Unique selling points (USPs) are the features of a product or service that make it special and will persuade people to buy or use it. Brochures emphasise the USPs for their target audience.

   a   Working with a partner, list all the USPs for your school that you think are appealing to pupils. This could include particular facilities, subjects, clubs, people, rooms or anything else that the school has to offer.

b Now repeat the activity but this time don't think as a pupil – think as a parent. What are the appealing features of your school for parents?

c Compare and contrast the two lists you have made. Are there any USPs that will appeal to both pupils and parents? What differences are there between the two lists? If you were creating a persuasive brochure about your school, deciding on its audience – pupils or parents – would help you decide which USPs to include when writing the brochure.

Give it a go!

Your school is producing a brochure to promote the school to new pupils. The headteacher has asked your class to write the text for part of the brochure, persuading new pupils to get involved in as many extra-curricular activities as possible. Your class has been sent the following memo:

> From: The headteacher
>
> Thank you for agreeing to help produce this year's school brochure. We are asking different classes to write sections of the brochure. Your class has been chosen to write about the extra-curricular activities we have on offer. Some of the pictures we want to include are provided here.

Write this section of the brochure, persuading pupils that getting involved in extra-curricular activities will help them to make the most of their time at school.

Working in a small group, look carefully at the information you have been given and answer the following questions, making brief notes:

- What is the purpose of the brochure?
- Who is the audience for the brochure?
- What sort of language and style would be suited to this audience?
- What **writers' techniques** do you think you will be using?
- What part of the brochure have you been asked to produce?
- What should be included in it as content?

Studying a brochure

The headteacher has received a brochure from another school and would be grateful for your opinion on this extract from it.

Welcome to

Langton Park School!

Get the most from your time at Langton Park School

If you thought that school was just about lessons, homework and exams, you were wrong. Here at Langton Park there are hundreds of other things for you to do which will help you to get the most out of your time here and fulfil your potential.

Try to get involved in as many activities as you can. The more you put into your time here, the more you will get out of it!

There are different activities, which will appeal to different people. Some are regular clubs which go on during a particular term, or during the whole year; others are one-off events which take place once a year or once in a lifetime!

Sport for all

Think you might be the next Wayne Rooney or Paula Radcliffe? Then there are lots of opportunities for you to get involved in sports and PE activities at this school. There are teams for all the major sports – football, hockey, rugby, basketball, athletics, to name but a few. There are also clubs for less well-known sports such as korfball and squash. Don't think you have to be brilliant, though. If you're interested, just come along and give it a go. It's taking part that matters, not necessarily being brilliant at everything. There are also less competitive sports and fitness activities on offer, such as aerobics and rowing. Check the PE noticeboard for what's on and when.

Arts 'n' crafts 'n' drama 'n' music

If sport isn't your thing, what about something arty? There is an art club for all years which gives you the opportunity to try all sorts of different techniques from pottery to graffiti art. Go on – try something you haven't done before!

If the stage is more your scene, what about joining the drama club, or auditioning for a part in one of the school productions? If actually appearing on stage makes you go cold with fear, but you are interested in being involved, what about helping backstage? There are always opportunities on the technical side.

Budding musicians also have lots of chances to express themselves and find fame at Langton Park. There are music groups, bands and choirs for all ages and all levels of ability. A willingness to take part and get involved is more important than being grade 8. Just come along to the first rehearsal in any term and give it a go.

Best of the rest

There are other opportunities for anyone who isn't into sport, art, drama or music. There is a computer club for you nerds out there, which runs Mondays, Wednesdays and Fridays in Computer Room 1.

During the year there will also be language days devoted to a modern foreign language, creative writing competitions for wannabe writers and science challenge activities for those of you addicted to experiments and all things scientific.

In the summer there is a charity week where everyone gets involved in all sorts of mad activities to raise money for your favourite charities. Then don't forget the good old resource centre which is open every day for books, CDs and much, much more.

What are you going to do?

So, you can see there is no need ever to be bored at lunchtime. Listen out in assemblies and check noticeboards regularly. Take advantage of everything that's on offer and don't be afraid to give something new a go.

Remember, the more you put into your time here, the more you will get out of it!

Using different types of sentences

1 a Read the text of the brochure and pick out three examples of each of the following:

- sentences with direct instructions to the reader
- rhetorical questions
- exclamations
- sentences that contain relative clauses (clauses beginning with 'which' or 'who').

b Think about the sentences you have identified and answer the following questions:

- Why does the writer use a mixture of sentence types in the brochure?
- What is the **effect on the reader** of being given instructions and asked questions?
- Why does the writer use exclamations?
- How does the use of relative clauses help the writer to give the reader lots of information?

Paragraphs and links

2 Persuasive texts usually contain a series of linked points that all support one particular viewpoint. To guide the reader through the text, writers create textual cohesion by linking paragraphs together in a variety of ways.

a One way of doing this is by using repetition. Re-read the Langton Park School brochure and find a phrase that is repeated in the first and second paragraphs, and a different phrase that is repeated in the second and fourth paragraphs.

b The writer also uses references back to information mentioned earlier in the text to create cohesion. How is the paragraph describing art and drama linked to the paragraph describing sport? How is the paragraph introducing the computer clubs linked to the previous paragraphs?

Using different text types

3 This brochure is aimed at new pupils and uses language that is appropriate for young people. In pairs, discuss the ways in which this brochure tries to appeal to its target audience. Think about:

- the opening and ending
- how the reader is addressed in the text
- the use of slogans
- the order in which things are mentioned
- the use of words and phrases that reflect the language of young people.

4 To emphasise the key persuasive points and take into account the needs of their readers, writers of brochures **use a range of persuasive techniques**.

    a Some of the techniques used in the Langton Park School brochure are listed below. Copy and complete the table by picking out examples of each of these techniques.

Purpose	Technique	Example
Emphasise key persuasive points	Exaggeration	'find fame at Langton Park'
	Examples to illustrate points	
	Repetition of key words or ideas	
	Rhetorical questions	
Take into account the reader's needs	Directly addressing the reader	'If you thought that school was just about lessons'
	Appealing to the reader's emotions	
	Links to the reader's personal experiences	
	Anticipate objections	

    b How effective do you think these **writers' techniques** will be in persuading the reader?

Planning to write

Organising the ideas

1 **a** Look back at the notes you made about the task on page 11. Add any other ideas you have after reading the Langton Park School brochure.

    b Copy and complete the planning frame below to help you structure the text for your brochure. You should start each paragraph with a topic sentence stating the main point and the rest of the paragraph should add information to this. Your introduction and conclusion should be linked to reinforce your persuasive message.

Introduction	Key points:
Paragraph 1	Sub-heading: Key point for topic sentence: Additional information:
Conclusion	Key points: Link back to introduction:

2 **Write for a reader**. Decide what sort of language would be appropriate for your audience and jot down any words and phrases that might appeal to your readers and be effective in persuading them.

Composing

Using different types of sentences

1 Now start to write the text for your section of the brochure.

a Think about the persuasive techniques you explored in the Langton Park School brochure. Try to **use the following writers' techniques** to emphasise your persuasive points:

- illustrating points with examples
- exaggeration
- repetition
- rhetorical questions
- humour
- directly addressing the reader
- unusual language.

b Remember to **rehearse sentences in your head**. As you link your ideas into sentences, say them aloud or imagine how they would sound. Do they sound persuasive? Is the language appropriate for your audience?

Improving

Using different text types

1 When you have finished drafting your text, re-read each section and decide whether you have used language that will appeal to your target audience. What techniques have you used to do this? Are there any other **writers' techniques** you could use?

2 **Think about the effect on the reader**. Imagine yourself as the audience of this text. Would it appeal to you? Are there any parts of the text where you could make **changes** to:

- directly address the reader
- appeal to the reader's emotions
- link your ideas to the reader's own experiences
- anticipate objections and try to win the reader over?

▶ Reviewing

1 Work in a group of four, divided into two pairs.
- One pair should act as editors and proof-readers, checking each piece of work to make sure that what you have written is accurately spelled and punctuated and makes sense. Identify any errors and suggest corrections.
- One pair should analyse each brochure text and prepare an oral report for the headteacher about the strengths of each one and how it persuades its audience.

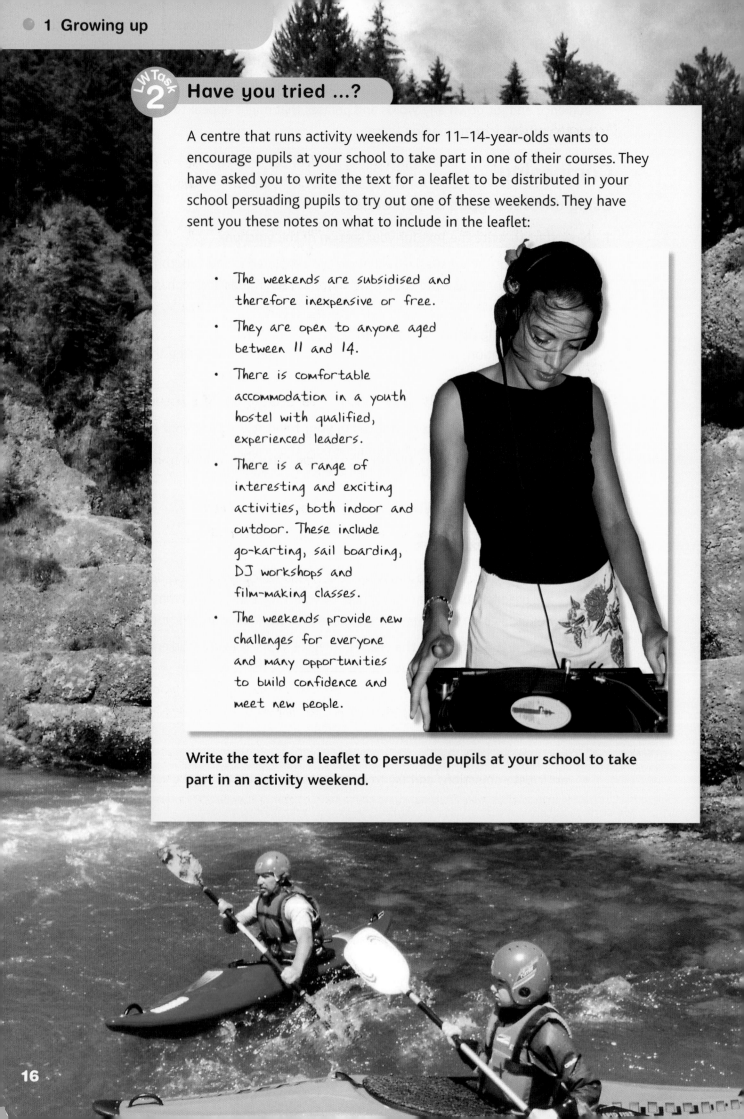

Have you tried ...?

A centre that runs activity weekends for 11–14-year-olds wants to encourage pupils at your school to take part in one of their courses. They have asked you to write the text for a leaflet to be distributed in your school persuading pupils to try out one of these weekends. They have sent you these notes on what to include in the leaflet:

- The weekends are subsidised and therefore inexpensive or free.
- They are open to anyone aged between 11 and 14.
- There is comfortable accommodation in a youth hostel with qualified, experienced leaders.
- There is a range of interesting and exciting activities, both indoor and outdoor. These include go-karting, sail boarding, DJ workshops and film-making classes.
- The weekends provide new challenges for everyone and many opportunities to build confidence and meet new people.

Write the text for a leaflet to persuade pupils at your school to take part in an activity weekend.

Planning to write

Organising the ideas

1 a What is the purpose and audience of this leaflet? Look back at the questions at the bottom of page 11 to remind yourself of the factors you will need to consider when completing this task.

  b **Write for a reader.** Working with a partner, list all the USPs of the activity weekend that would appeal to teenagers. Add your own ideas to those provided by the activity centre.

2 Now plan the sections of your text. You could use a planning frame like the one you used for Task 1 on page 14.

Composing

Using different text types and using different types of sentences

1 Remember to use the strategies you have already worked on:

- **Write for a reader** and think about how you can address them using appropriate language.

- **Use the persuasive writers' techniques** you have explored.

- **Rehearse sentences in your head** and experiment with different types of sentences.

- **Change** what you have written to explore different **effects on the reader**.

Improving

Using different text types

1 a Re-read your writing. Would it be effective in persuading young people to try out an activity weekend? What **persuasive techniques** have you used to appeal to your audience?

  b Identify places where you could use other persuasive techniques to make the text more successful. Look back at the techniques used to emphasise persuasive points and to take into account the needs of the reader listed on page 14.

▶ Reviewing

1 Return to your plan. Have you included everything you wanted to include? Have you used a range of **persuasive techniques** effectively to:

- emphasise key persuasive points
- take into account the reader's needs?

2 Set yourself one key target you will try to achieve next time you write a persuasive text.

② Emergencies

Inform, explain, describe

When you are writing to inform, explain and describe, it is important to present factual information so that it is easy for the reader or listener to follow and understand what you are saying. In this unit you will write a speech that explains information clearly to an audience and uses an appropriate tone. You will explore how to organise your sentences so that ideas are stated clearly and directly and details are added concisely.

Writing strategies

- write for a reader
- rehearse sentences in your head
- loop back
- changing

Pre-writing: write for a reader

When writing a speech, it is important to plan very carefully what you want to say and how you will say it, thinking about your audience.

1 In a small group, discuss presentations that you have heard. These may have been in assembly, or from a visiting speaker. How did the speaker catch your attention and hold it throughout the speech? What techniques did they use to let you know what the talk was about?

2 a Effective speakers focus on helping the audience to get the most out of their speech and use a range of techniques to do this. Some of these techniques are listed below. Copy and complete this table by matching each of the techniques to the reasons speakers use them. Some techniques are used for more than one reason and so might fit under more than one heading.

Engage and keep the audience's attention	Let the audience know what the speech will be about	Use an appropriate tone	Speak directly to the audience

Techniques:
- Show understanding of how the audience is feeling (empathise)
- Start the speech with a short overview of the content
- Use sentences of different lengths
- Use personal pronouns, such as 'you'
- Put the main idea at the start of the sentence
- Make the audience feel welcome
- Use a range of punctuation to communicate ideas clearly
- Use a variety of sentence openings
- Use alternative words (synonyms) rather than repeating the same one
- Tell the audience what each section is going to be about
- Use a variety of ways of joining ideas in sentences
- Use formal expressions.

b Use coloured pens to annotate your completed table with traffic lights colour-coding to show how confident you are at using each technique yourself:

- Red: you are not confident about using this technique
- Amber: you are fairly confident about trying this technique
- Green: you are confident you can use this technique successfully.

You will practise using these techniques in this unit so that you will be able to use more of them confidently.

Safety first

You are a teacher and have planned a school camping trip for a group of pupils. The headteacher has asked you to speak to parents before the trip to explain what steps have been taken to ensure that their children will be safe. The concerns that have been raised by parents are:

- What if someone is taken ill or has an accident in the middle of nowhere?
- Will my child get enough to eat? If she's left to fend for herself, she'll starve!
- I know the students will be doing some things on their own, but what if something goes wrong?

Write a speech to parents explaining what has been done to make sure that their children will be safe on this camping trip.

The explanations given to parents should be clear and simple, convincing them that steps are being taken to ensure that their children will be safe. The speaker must decide whether to organise the information in order of importance or by explaining things in the order in which they will happen. The style should be semi-formal to reassure parents that their concerns are being taken seriously and information should be presented concisely and accurately to make it easy to understand.

Studying a speech

Using different types of sentences

1 Below is the opening of the speech, which has been prepared for you by the headteacher. How effective do you think this opening would be? Think back to the techniques you discussed in the pre-writing task on page 19 and answer these questions:

- Does the opening catch your attention?
- Does the speaker start by saying what they are talking about?
- Is there anything that seems odd as you read it?

> We will be asking the parents to guarantee that the children are fit at the beginning of the trip and we will monitor the children to ensure that no children are becoming tired or overstretched. We will allow breaks during treks and the children will eat healthily. We will be taking snacks to keep the children going and all the leaders are trained and I have taken additional training in dealing with emergencies. We will be able to administer treatment to the children and local services have been alerted and will be on hand to assist should it be necessary to get further medical attention for anyone or transport the children to hospital.

2 a One of the problems with this opening is that the writer has used too many similarly constructed sentences. Investigate this by identifying:

- the way each sentence starts
- the length of each sentence
- the way the writer joins ideas in each sentence.

b What do you notice about the range of sentences used? What problems could this cause? What recommendations could you make to the headteacher to improve the opening?

21

3 a The headteacher has now revised the opening of the speech in response to your recommendations. Below is a copy of the new version which has been annotated to describe the techniques that have been used to make improvements. Working with a partner, read through the annotations and discuss the techniques that have been used in this version of the opening.

b With your partner, discuss how effectively this version of the speech:

- lets the audience know what the speech will be about
- engages the audience's attention at the start
- speaks directly to the audience.

> Starts with a phrase that organises the information for the audience.

> The writer replaces 'trip' with 'experience', which has a similar meaning (a synonym).

> The opening of the sentence tells the audience what the paragraph will be about.

> Sentence starts with a phrase before the main subject and verb ('we will').

First of all, I want to say thank you to all you parents who are supporting this trip. Without you, it wouldn't be possible – and I know your children are going to benefit from the experience.

I realise that some of you may have some anxieties about some aspects of the trip and I want to explain the steps we have taken to ensure that the trip is as safe as possible in every way.

In terms of the physical safety of students, we will be asking you to guarantee that they are fit at the beginning of the trip. We will monitor everyone closely to ensure that no one is becoming unduly tired or overstretched. There will be regular breaks during treks and students will be encouraged to eat healthily. We will be taking high-energy snacks such as dried fruit and nuts to keep them going. All the leaders are first-aid trained and I have taken additional training in dealing with medical emergencies away from civilisation. In the unlikely event of an emergency, we will be able to administer treatment to students. Local emergency services have been alerted and will be on hand to assist should it be necessary to get further medical attention for anyone or transport them to hospital.

> Engages the audience by making them feel appreciated.

> The writer uses the pronoun 'it' to refer to the trip.

> Gives an overview of the content linked to the purpose of the speech.

> Compound sentence: two sentences are linked by 'and'. We often use compound sentences when we speak.

4 How would you describe the tone of the opening? Choose from these words or think of some of your own.

- formal
- friendly
- reassuring
- informal
- sincere

5 Working with a partner, read the rest of the speech below. As you read it, note how the writer uses:

- different ways of starting sentences, for example, phrases such as 'In terms of'
- a variety of ways of joining ideas in sentences, for example, conjunctions such as 'if'
- different sentence lengths.

6 Re-read the last paragraph of the speech. How effective do you think this ending would be? Think about the purpose of the speech and the effect that it would have on the audience.

Students will be going off in groups to carry out particular activities such as map-reading exercises. They will never be on their own, however; they will always be in groups of at least three people. Leaders will monitor pupils carefully to ensure only appropriate challenges are set and if, for example, there is a difficulty, such as adverse weather conditions, group exercises will be cancelled or modified accordingly. We are not encouraging the use of mobile phones, but they will be available as a last resort to provide necessary means of communication between groups and leaders.

In terms of diet, a list of nutritious foods has been drawn up for the expedition. Students will be taking the lead in allocating rations and cooking meals – this is part of the challenge of the trip. However, in the interests of the wellbeing and morale of the whole group, leaders included, we will step in if there is any danger of provisions being wasted or students not getting a proper balanced diet.

I hope these points reassure you that we have taken all possible steps to ensure the safety and wellbeing of your children during this expedition. If you have any further queries, please raise them now.

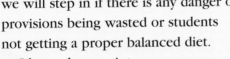

Range of punctuation

7 Using a range of punctuation effectively when writing a speech helps you to communicate ideas clearly to your audience.

a Commas are used to separate phrases and clauses in sentences. Re-read this sentence from the speech:

> Leaders will monitor pupils carefully to ensure only appropriate challenges are set and if, for example, there is a difficulty, such as adverse weather conditions, group exercises will be cancelled or modified accordingly.

Identify the two phrases that are separated off by using commas. Why has this technique been used to include extra information in the speech?

b Semi-colons can be used to show a close link between points. Try reading this sentence aloud:

> They will never be on their own, however; they will always be in groups of at least three people.

How does the semi-colon help to show the link between the points to the audience?

c In the following sentence a dash is used:

> Students will be taking the lead in allocating rations and cooking meals – this is part of the challenge of the trip.

What other punctuation could have been used instead of the dash? Why has the writer chosen to use a dash here?

d In pairs, re-read the whole speech focusing on the punctuation used. Pick out other sentences where punctuation is used to help the speaker express ideas clearly to the audience. You could try reading the speech aloud to decide the impact of each punctuation mark.

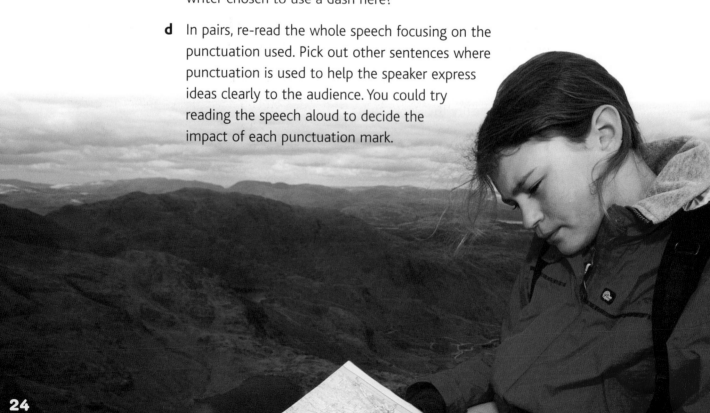

Planning to write

Interesting texts

1 **a** You are going to add a paragraph to the speech addressing another concern from parents. Working in a small group, decide on another issue that parents might want the teacher to respond to, for example pupils' behaviour or the cost of the trip.

  b Role-play the following situation: a group of anxious parents question the teacher about the concerns that they have. Before you begin, plan a series of questions to ask the teacher.

  c Copy out the note-making frame below which will help you organise your notes. Fill in the questions you are going to ask and then begin the role-play. Make notes on how the teacher responds to your questions in the second column.

Parents' questions	Teacher's comments

Composing

Using different types of sentences

1 **a** You are now going to use your notes to write a paragraph to add to the speech. Your paragraph should address the concern you focused on in your role-play. Remember that you need to **write for the audience** and:

- anticipate the concerns parents may have
- make the information clear
- convince parents that there won't be any problems.

Before you begin to write, remind yourself of the different techniques you have studied in this unit to help communicate your ideas effectively.

  b Working individually, write a draft of your paragraph.

- Start by stating the issue. For example, you could use the opening, 'In order to ensure students behave well, we will ...'. What other paragraph openings can you think of?
- Then add several pieces of information for parents. Don't forget to think of synonyms to keep your writing interesting.
- As you write, **rehearse sentences in your head** before you write them down to check how they will sound to the audience.
- Remember to use different sentence structures and sentence lengths. Make sure you start your sentences in different ways.
- Use different ways of linking your ideas together. What punctuation could you use instead of the word 'and'?
- As you write, use the **looping back** writing strategy. Before you construct the next sentence, re-read what you have written, with the audience in mind, to check that your points are clearly explained, expressed in an interesting way and that you have included the information the listener needs.

▶ Reviewing

1 a Swap your paragraph with a partner. Read your partner's draft and annotate it to show how the techniques you have been studying in this unit have been used. Are there any places in your partner's paragraph where you can write the following statements?

- Clear opening sentence telling the listener what the paragraph is about
- Contrasting sentence openings
- Different sentence structures
- Varied sentence lengths
- Ideas linked by using a word other than 'and'
- Punctuation that helps to make the meaning clear.

b Discuss the annotations you have made with your partner.

- Which techniques have they used successfully?
- Which ones do they need to try next time? Can you show them any places where they could have used these?

SW Task 2 Antarctic emergencies

You are taking an inexperienced group of people on a dangerous mission to the Antarctic. There have been suggestions that this trip is foolhardy and involves taking unnecessary risks. You have been asked to write a press statement that will be presented to journalists at a televised news conference, explaining the plans you have made to deal with each of the emergencies that you could face.

These are the main emergencies likely to be faced:
- attacks by killer seals
- violent snowstorms
- running short of food and drink.

Write the press statement explaining the plans you have made to deal with any emergencies.

This press statement has two audiences: people who will see the news conference on television and journalists who will use your explanations as a basis for their reports. What elements of structure and style can you use to ensure that your explanations will be effective in convincing these audiences that the expedition is worthwhile?

Planning to write

Interesting texts

1 Working with a partner, make brief notes on how you could deal with each emergency listed in the task. Think about these questions:

- What equipment will you have to help you in each situation?
- Will you be able to communicate with rescuers?
- What have you done to train the group in basic procedures?

You could also use the Internet to research what real explorers might do in similar situations.

2 Think about how you are going to start and end your press statement. How can the opening and ending help you to communicate your ideas to your audience?

Composing

Using different types of sentences

1 **a** Individually, draft your press statement, remembering to **write for the audience**. What do you need to do to help your listeners understand what you are saying and remain interested?

b What tone do you want to use for this press statement? Think carefully about who the audience is and the techniques you should use to create the appropriate tone. Look back to the pre-writing task on page 19 to help you.

2 As you write, keep **looping back** to check that your sentences follow on logically from each other, and give yourself time to think about how to link your ideas together. Remember also to focus on variety in sentence openings and length. It will help if you **rehearse your sentences in your head**.

Range of punctuation

3 **a** Check that you have used a range of punctuation effectively to help the audience to understand the information given. If you are not sure what the effect of the punctuation you have used will be, experiment by reading your sentences aloud.

b Are there any other ways that you could use punctuation to help communicate your ideas to the audience? For example, could it add emphasis or help you present your ideas more concisely? What **changes** could you make?

Improving

Interesting texts

1 **a** Read the draft of your press statement aloud to a partner. Together discuss the following questions:

- Did it engage the listener and keep their attention?
- Was the information presented clearly?
- Was the tone appropriate for the audience?

b Discuss how you could **change** any parts of your statement to make it more effective. Work together to make the necessary changes.

▶ Reviewing

1 a At the beginning of this unit, you thought about how confident you felt about the different techniques you can use to write a speech. Copy and complete the following table to record which of these techniques you have now used in your own writing.

- Red: you have not used this technique in your writing
- Amber: you have used this technique a little
- Green: you have used this technique throughout your writing.

	Techniques	Have I used this?		
		Red	Amber	Green
Engage and keep the audience's attention	Synonyms			
	A variety of sentence openings			
	Sentences that are different lengths			
	A variety of ways of joining ideas in sentences			
Let the audience know what the speech will be about	Starting with a short overview of the content			
	Introducing each section			
	Main idea at the start of the sentence			
Use an appropriate tone	Formal expressions			
	Empathising			
	A range of punctuation to communicate ideas clearly			
Speak directly to the audience	Personal pronouns			
	Making the audience feel welcome			

b Look back at which of these techniques you felt able to use confidently in the pre-writing task on page 19. What progress have you made in this unit? Think about which techniques you are now able to use that you had not used before.

c Now focus on the techniques you have not used or have used only a little. Check that you understand how and when to use these techniques. These are areas for you to improve next time.

Healthy eating

Analyse, review, comment

When you are writing to analyse, review and comment, it is important to communicate your own opinions to the reader, even if your writing discusses both sides of the issue. In this unit you will comment on healthy eating proposals, exploring how to use words as signposts to guide the reader through the text and how to structure the beginning and ending of your writing effectively.

Writing strategies

- use writers' techniques
- think about the effect on the reader

Pre-writing: use writers' techniques

1 **a** In this unit, you will be writing about ways to encourage healthy eating. Read Task 1 on page 30 and look at the proposed new laws. Working in a small group, choose one of the proposals. In your group, discuss the following questions:

- What do you think of the proposed new law?

- Do you think it would be successful? Where would you put it on the following scale?

Not successful ——————————————— Very successful

- Why did you choose to put it at this point? Make a note of all the reasons you have. Start with 'because' and think of some different reasons.

b You now need to share your group's opinions with the class. Choose one member of the group to feed back. Make notes on the other groups' ideas too as you will use these later in the unit.

'Bad' foods banned!

You are a journalist who writes about health issues. The following new laws have just been proposed to encourage people to eat more healthily:

- the number of fast-food restaurants to be restricted in any one area

- some high-fat or high-sugar foods to carry a health warning

- certain high-fat foods such as burgers and ice-cream to be taxed, to make them more expensive

- butter, cheese, cream and chocolate to be rationed

- information about the fat, sugar and salt content of all food products to be displayed prominently in large print on packaging.

Write an article for a national newspaper commenting on these proposed new laws.

Look again at the writing task and think about:

- Purpose – to comment on the proposed new laws, making your own viewpoint clear to readers.

- Audience – a national audience, including both teenagers and adults.

- Structure – the opening should explain the issues you are going to comment on. Then the article should move on to develop your point of view, backing this up with evidence. The last paragraph should conclude the article, either summarising your main points or asking the reader to think about the issues.

- Style – you need to decide where your article is going to appear. For some newspapers, like *The Times*, the style should be quite serious and formal, but for others, such as the *Mirror*, it should be more light-hearted and chatty.

Studying a newspaper article

Paragraphs and links

The way a writer on a newspaper begins and ends their writing is crucial. The best writing should have a strong opening that engages the reader's attention. The ending should leave the reader with something to think about. Good writers make sure there are links between the beginning and the ending.

1 In pairs, read the following two paragraphs at the top of page 31. Can you work out which is the opening and which is the ending of a newspaper article?

   a Discuss which one is the opening paragraph and the evidence that shows this. How does the writer let the reader know it is the beginning?

   b Now think about the ending. What signals are there that this paragraph is the end of the writing?

   c How do you know that these paragraphs come from the same piece of writing? What links are there between the opening paragraph and the ending paragraph?

Obviously, the health of the nation is an important matter: one the Government has to take seriously. Obesity is a growing problem and, for the first time in years, our predicted lifespan is no longer increasing. Something has to be done. A programme of education has been in place for some time, encouraging people to eat more fresh food, particularly fruit and vegetables. It has even been the topic of popular television programmes such as 'You are what you eat'. But this has not had the impact the Government would have liked. The proposals published yesterday go one step further in trying to persuade us to eat more healthily. They are desperate measures for what some regard as a desperate situation.

So, to conclude, these are probably useful measures to help us to improve the balance of what we eat and ensure that the diet of the nation is a healthy one. But apart from this, the proposed new laws won't work: if encouragement to eat more fruit and vegetables did not work, undoubtedly enforcement will not work either. In the end, people have to be informed with the best nutritional advice, expected to make sensible decisions and left to get on with it. There will be no end to this desperate situation unless people realise for themselves that 'they are what they eat'.

2 You are now going to explore the different **writers' techniques** used in the opening and ending paragraphs. Copy and complete the following table by providing the missing definitions and purposes for each of the techniques. You should also pick out examples of the use of each technique from the opening and ending paragraphs.

Technique	Definition	Purpose	Example from opening paragraph	Example from ending paragraph
Adverbs		To add an emphasis to particular ideas	Obviously	Undoubtedly
Repetition	Where a word or phrase is used more than once			
Connectives	Words that link sentences or introduce another point		But	

Refer back to your completed table when you need to remind yourself about the **techniques** you can use in your own writing to make effective links between two paragraphs or between sentences.

Now read the complete newspaper article from which the opening and ending paragraphs were taken.

'Bad' foods banned

Obviously, the health of the nation is an important matter: one the Government has to take seriously. Obesity is a growing problem and, for the first time in years, our predicted lifespan is no longer increasing. Something has to be done. A programme of education has been in place for some time, encouraging people to eat more fresh food, particularly fruit and vegetables. It has even been the topic of popular television programmes such as 'You are what you eat'. But this has not had the impact the Government would have liked. The proposals published yesterday go one step further in trying to persuade us to eat more healthily. They are desperate measures for what some regard as a desperate situation.

So what has been proposed? Well, it's almost the opposite of the situation during the war. Then, when food was scarce, it was rationed so people got a fair share of what was available. Now, because we have an abundance of food, it is going to be rationed to stop us eating too much of it. These proposals aim to make it more difficult to get hold of the food we all seem to love: high-fat, high-sugar, high-salt food which is quick and easy to buy and to eat. It's going to be harder and more expensive to find and we are going to be reminded constantly that it's BAD for us.

There are two main questions to be asked: the first is 'will these proposals work?' and the second is 'are they practical and realistic in Britain?' In the first case, I am not sure. They will certainly make people more aware of the dangers of eating a diet that is unhealthy. The higher cost in particular will put some people off as will the need to fiddle about with ration books. At the same time, for some people it will make these wicked, prohibited foods even more desirable. I imagine some burger junkies going to all sorts of lengths to find a burger joint, chocoholics going underground to get hold of it on the black market and whole crime rackets building up around people's craving for the hard stuff – freshly cooked chips glistening with oil and salt, followed by deep-fried Mars bars.

Then there is the cost of putting these measures in place. What happens to all those people currently employed in the food industry producing ready-meals groaning with evil ingredients? What happens to all the people

currently working in burger bars and pizza joints? Who is going to employ them now? Then there is the cost of setting up a rationing system. This is going to be complicated and almost impossible to administer. What exactly is going to be rationed – all chocolate or just milk chocolate? Everything with chocolate in it, even chocolate chips? Who decides anyway? Given the huge range of food products available in the 21st century, it is impossible to come up with a system of rationing that is fair and workable.

Limiting the quantities of sugar, fat and salt that go into food, particularly those aimed at children or provided in school canteens, could, however, be both fair and effective as a means of reducing our intake of these substances. If children are taught about these foods in schools as well, this will help to educate us about what we should be eating and protect those who aren't yet old enough to take full responsibility for their own diets.

So, to conclude, these are probably useful measures to help us to improve the balance of what we eat and ensure that the diet of the nation is a healthy one. But apart from this, the proposed new laws won't work: if encouragement to eat more fruit and vegetables did not work, undoubtedly enforcement will not work either. In the end, people have to be informed with the best nutritional advice, expected to make sensible decisions and left to get on with it. There will be no end to this desperate situation unless people realise for themselves that 'they are what they eat'.

Choice of vocabulary

3 Working in a pair, close read the newspaper article. Pick out any key words you can find that give the reader a clue about the opinion of the author. For example, 'BAD' in the second paragraph.

4 Now look closely at the second paragraph.

    a Why do you think the writer uses 'we' and 'us'?

    b How has the writer used adjectives to condense the information when writing about 'food'?

5 Re-read the third and fourth paragraphs.

    a What is the main idea of each of these paragraphs? Think of an appropriate sub-heading for each paragraph.

    b Look at how the writer has added extra detail to the nouns chosen through the use of expanded noun phrases, such as 'freshly cooked chips glistening with oil and salt'. What do you think the writer is trying to make the reader think?

6 Look again at the final paragraph. How does it balance all the ideas that have been introduced in the article?

Planning to write

Organising the ideas

1 Look back at the notes you made in the pre-writing task on page 29. After reading the newspaper article commenting on these proposed new laws, are there any other ideas you can add to your notes?

2 Use a fishbone plan to collect together all the ideas from your notes. You will use this to help you to write your own newspaper article commenting on the proposed new laws. Following the example shown below, put each proposal along one of the bones, then add the reasons it would or would not be successful.

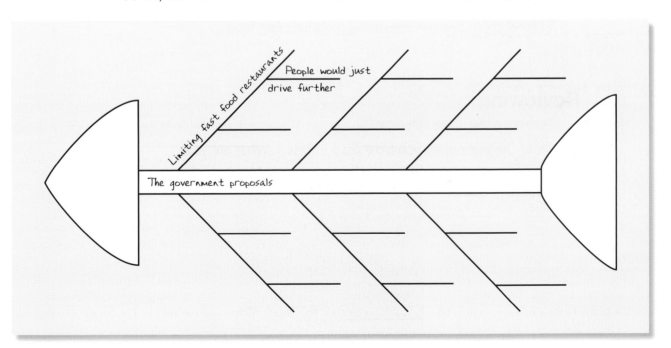

Composing

Paragraphs and links

1 a You are now going to plan and draft the opening and ending paragraphs of your article. Plan these paragraphs and annotate your plan to show how you are going to **use the writers' techniques** you have studied. Look back at your completed version of the table on page 31 to remind yourself of these.

  b Then write the first draft. When you have completed this, ask your partner to read it and underline the techniques you have included to engage the reader and make links between the opening and the ending.

2 Now decide on the opening sentences of each of the middle paragraphs. Remember to **think about the effect on the reader**. Pick one main idea from your plan and write it into sentence form. Make sure you include connecting adverbs that help introduce each section. You could use connectives such as 'Firstly', 'Additionally', 'Furthermore' and 'Moreover' as ways of introducing your middle paragraphs. Try putting these connectives within the sentence instead of always at the start.

3 Now draft your article, remembering to **use writers' techniques**. Use adverbs for emphasis, such as 'obviously', 'clearly' and 'undoubtedly' to strengthen your comments.

4 As you draft, refer back to your completed table of **writers' techniques** to help you check that you are linking your paragraphs effectively.

Improving

Choice of vocabulary

1 Swap your draft article with a partner. Ask your partner to spend ten minutes underlining any nouns they can find in your writing. When you get your work back, check to see whether you could make any of these into expanded noun phrases, so that you can add some extra comment through your word choice. For instance, 'fast food' could become 'irresistible, delicious fast food'.

▶ Reviewing

1 Think about the techniques you have used in Task 1. What are your strengths and weaknesses? Set yourself two personal targets that you will try to achieve in Task 2.

Healthy eating for all

In response to the recent high profile of obesity and the problems associated with unhealthy eating habits, the governors at your school have decided that things need to change in the canteen.

The governors have proposed the following changes to the provision of food in your school:

- The vending machines/tuck shop should sell only plain water/juice and healthy snacks, such as dried fruit.

- The school canteen should provide low-fat, low-sugar, low-salt food only, e.g. no chips, burgers, doughnuts or cookies.

- Only brown rolls and wholemeal pasta and rice should be included in school meals.

- Puddings and cakes should be replaced by fruit and yoghurt.

- A committee of students should be set up to review canteen meals and make suggestions to the canteen staff.

- Students should be encouraged to bring healthy packed lunches.

Write an article for the school newspaper commenting on the advantages and disadvantages of these proposals and giving your opinion.

Planning to write

Organising the ideas

1 Remember to think about the purpose and audience of this article. How should you structure your writing? What style will be appropriate?

2 Spend some time thinking about the governors' proposals. Look back at the questions you discussed in the pre-writing task on page 29 and apply them to these proposals.

3 Make a bank of words, phrases and techniques you used in Task 1 that you could use again in this one. Remember, you can take some of the most successful words and ideas from the first article to use or improve on in the second.

4 Now think about your plan. **Use writers' techniques** from the first writing task to help you think about some of the things you could include. Refer back to the table on page 31 and try to include as many of these techniques as possible in your plan. Plan how you will open your article. Plan the ending as well, jotting down the links you could make between the opening paragraph and the concluding one.

Composing

Paragraphs and links

1 **Think about the effect on the reader**. Plan the connectives you are going to use, and the opening sentences for each paragraph before you begin writing so that your reader can follow your writing easily. As you draft your article, make sure that you take your time and that you keep referring back to your plan.

2 Use a variety of ways of linking your ideas: connectives are one way, but the writer used many others in the model text on page 32. Are there any of these methods you could use yourself?

▶ Reviewing

1 When you have completed your article, check how successfully you have **used writers' techniques**. Using a variety of different colours, highlight the links you have made between your opening and ending. Annotate them to explain the links you made. Finally, write one sentence in the margin saying what you wanted the reader to think and feel as they read each paragraph, drawing arrows to the places you expected this to happen.

2 Copy and complete the following table to help you set targets for your future work on grouping and linking paragraphs. Add to the table any other techniques you explored in Task 1 that you then went on to use in Task 2.

Technique	I am good at	I tried for the first time	I will use next time
Choosing a helpful planning format			
Putting key words and connectives into my plan			
Organising my opening			
Linking to the next paragraph			
Using connectives			
Linking the beginning and the ending			
Organising my ending			
Adding a concluding statement			

4 Saving animals

Imagine, explore, entertain

When you are writing to imagine, explore and entertain, you need to use all your senses to create a clear picture in your head of what you are describing to the reader. In this unit you will imagine an event and learn how to choose vocabulary to help bring your ideas alive as well as considering the spelling strategies that will help you to use this vocabulary accurately. You will also look at the ways a writer can show the reader the narrator's viewpoint effectively.

Writing strategies

- substituting
- think about the effect on the reader
- adding
- stick to the objectives

Pre-writing: substituting

1 a Synonyms are words that have similar meanings and are used to avoid repetition and add interest. In groups of three, use a thesaurus to make a list of synonyms for the words 'exciting' and 'boring'.

b In your group, role-play the following situation: you and your friend are waiting in a long queue to meet a celebrity. In turn, speak your thoughts aloud – one of you should communicate how excited you are and the other how bored you are. The third member of the group should note down the words and phrases you use to show your feelings of boredom and excitement.

c Look back at your list of synonyms. Tick those that you used and add to your list any new words you used. Did you use any other phrases or comparisons (for example, 'I was so excited I felt like ...')? Add these to your list.

d Keeping a learning diary helps you to keep track of your progress. In your learning diary, record what you have learned about synonyms in this activity.

SW Task 1 The last tiger

Some people keep personal journals or diaries to record events in their lives and their thoughts and feelings about them. Looking back at a journal entry can help the writer to relive the event described and can also help other readers to understand the writer's experiences and their feelings about them.

Imagine that tigers have nearly died out as a species. There is only one tiger left in the world.

- This tiger is kept in a zoo.

- Imagine you go to visit this tiger with your class.

- There is a long queue to see him but this might be your only chance to see a real tiger ...

Your teacher has asked the class to imagine the experience of seeing the last tiger and to write a journal entry about it.

The purpose of this journal entry is to draw the reader into this imaginary experience so that they understand what the writer saw and how they felt. It will be important to think about the order that events are presented in, how to use pace to convey the excitement of the experience to the reader and how to use description to help the reader imagine the setting. The journal entry will be written in the first person (using 'I'), but remember that you are imagining the experience so the narrative voice is not your own. What viewpoint will your imaginary narrator have about the experience?

Studying a journal entry

Look at this journal entry about the experience written by a member of the class. Unfortunately, some of the words are difficult to read because the journal has been damaged. As you read the journal entry, think about how language is used to help the reader to imagine the experience of visiting the last tiger.

Queuing seemed to go on for ever. For ages nobody moved at all. We were standing behind a family of four, mum, dad and two children. It was the dad who wanted to see the tiger; the mum wanted to go for a cup of tea and the two children were ▬▬▬▬▬[1]

It was my dad who made me go. He said I'd never have another opportunity. The tiger was getting old now and probably wouldn't live much longer. When he died there would be no more. I'd never be able to see a real tiger, only pictures. When I thought about it, I wanted to see it too, perhaps so I could tell my children that I had seen the last tiger.

Eventually we _____[2] closer to the enclosure. The first thing I was aware of was the smell; it was like an exaggerated smell of animals, a smell of wildness and muscle, jungle and savannah. And I thought of the poor old tiger dying so far away from its homeland in a _____[3] pen, in a dull part of suburban England.

As we got closer to the entrance, the sense of anticipation began to rise. We could hear the excited comments of people in front of us, even the whingeing children, as they caught their first glimpse of the tiger. People started to push a little, anxious to move forward to see the tiger for themselves.

Then we were in the enclosure and I started leaning and pushing myself. I could feel my dad next to me also pushing forward. And then I saw it, the smooth tawny rump of the beast, just at the edge of my sight. I could feel myself stop breathing.

Gradually the full length of the tiger's body came into view and I could see

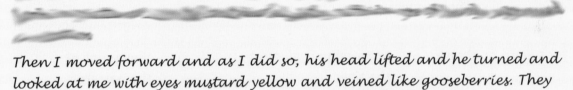

Then I moved forward and as I did so, his head lifted and he turned and looked at me with eyes mustard yellow and veined like gooseberries. They were as ancient as _____[4] and in them were boredom and _____[5] and deep, deep fury. And as I looked into his eyes he seemed to be looking directly at me as if to say 'You are to blame for this – it is you I hold responsible.' For a moment I wanted to rip open the door of the pen and let the tiger go free. Then the moment was over. I felt pressure from behind and our time with the tiger was over.

Choice of vocabulary

1   Writers choose their words carefully to show their own thoughts and feelings or those of their narrators towards the subject they are writing about. Copy and complete the following table. For each quotation from the journal entry, identify the impression it gives of the tiger and explain what this suggests about the narrator's viewpoint about the tiger and its situation. The first example has been completed for you.

Writer's word or phrase	Impression it gives of the tiger	Viewpoint of the narrator
'exaggerated smell of animals'	A strong mixture of smells – made worse because it's in a cage	Dislikes the smell
'poor old tiger dying so far away from its homeland'		
'beast'		
'eyes mustard yellow and veined like gooseberries'		

2   In small groups, re-read the journal entry and suggest a range of words that could fill each of the numbered gaps where the original has been damaged. Select your best idea for each gap and explain the **effect you want to create for the reader**.

3   a   The writer of the journal often shows the reader the narrator's growing sense of excitement and anticipation by selecting vocabulary that implies the viewpoint, rather than stating it directly. Looking carefully at the writer's choice of vocabulary, re-read the journal entry and pick out quotations from each paragraph that show the narrator's attitude towards the experience of visiting the tiger.

    b   Copy and complete the graph opposite to show how high the level of excitement is in each paragraph. Choose one quotation for each paragraph that shows this and briefly explain the **effect** each quotation has **on the reader**.

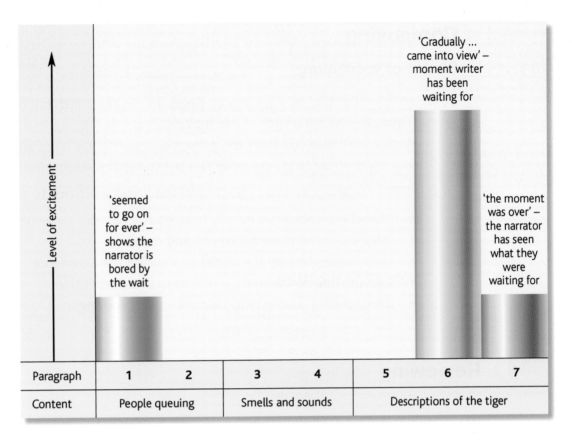

Paragraph	1	2	3	4	5	6	7
Content	People queuing		Smells and sounds		Descriptions of the tiger		

4 One technique used by writers to describe things is to **add** adjectives to the noun. The writer of this journal entry sometimes uses two adjectives together to form an expanded noun phrase, for example:

(adjectives) ——▶ [poor, old] [tiger] ◀—— (noun)

a Pick out any other examples you can find of the writer **adding** two adjectives to a noun in the journal entry.

b Explain what the **effect on the reader** might be for each example.

Correct spelling

As you begin to use more adventurous vocabulary, you also need strategies for learning how to spell these new words so that you can use them with confidence.

5 What spelling strategies do you know? Can you add to this list of techniques?

- Remember a related word that will help you, e.g. 'electric/electrician'.
- Make up a memory trick, e.g. 'ne**cess**ary' – think of a shirt with one **c**ollar and two **s**leeves.
- Identify the tricky bit of the word and learn that, e.g. 'definite' = -ite ending.
-
-

6 Here are four other words from the journal entry that have complex spellings:

- whingeing
- anxious
- muscle
- ancient

In pairs, decide on one way of remembering the spelling of each.

Composing

Choice of vocabulary

1 a Look back at the journal entry on pages 38–39. The paragraph beginning 'Gradually the full length …' has most of its words missing. In a small group, discuss what else you think the writer could see at this point and what the tiger was doing. What language could you use to tell the reader about this?

b With your group, complete the rest of the paragraph. **Stick to the objectives**:

- choosing vocabulary carefully to make the narrator's viewpoint clear
- using expanded noun phrases to **add** detail
- using similes to help the reader to visualise the experience
- **substituting** words with synonyms to avoid repetition
- using spelling strategies to help with tricky spellings.

▶ Reviewing

1 Swap paragraphs with another group. Annotate their paragraph to identify which techniques they have used. Make notes to explain the **effect on the reader** of each of these techniques.

2 Review your own group's paragraph. In your learning diary, note down what techniques you have learned to use so that you can record your progress.

First sighting

You are an explorer who has been searching in the South American jungle for a very rare breed of parrot that has strangely coloured feathers and a very unusual cry.

- You have been looking for this parrot for a long time.
- You have almost given up hope.
- Then one day you hear that the parrot has been seen nearby …

Write a journal entry about your experience of seeing this parrot for the first time.

Planning to write

Choice of vocabulary

1 You are going to work in a group of three to write this journal entry. To help you **stick to the objectives**, as a group review the information in your learning diaries about the techniques you need to use as you compose your journal entry. What other techniques can you add to this list?

- Expanding nouns by **adding** adjectives to help the reader imagine what the parrot looks like

-

-

2 **a** You need to help the reader to imagine the experience of seeing this rare breed of parrot. Imagine that you are the explorer. In your group of three, draw a spider diagram of words and phrases to help you agree the content and narrator's viewpoint for each of the following sections of the journal entry:

- Section 1: the long wait to see the parrot

- Section 2: the first sighting of the parrot

- Section 3: close encounter as you see the parrot close up.

Remember that in sections 1 and 2 you need to show the reader your growing excitement as you wait for this important arrival.

b For each word in your mind map, think about whether there are any synonyms that you could use as **substitutes** so that you can avoid repetition in your writing, for example 'plumage' instead of 'feathers'. Use a thesaurus to help you think of different words. Add these to your plan.

Composing

Choice of vocabulary

1 In your group of three, you are each going to write part of the journal entry that you have planned about the experience of seeing the parrot. Decide which of the sections you will each write.

- Section 1: the long wait to see the parrot. Imagine that you are really there and try to convey to the reader the viewpoint you have agreed.

- Section 2: the first sighting of the parrot. Remember to make it clear to the reader how you feel about this moment.

- Section 3: close encounter as you see the parrot close up. Let the reader know how you feel now you have found what you were searching for.

Think about how you can present the narrator's viewpoint in an interesting way. Remember that in the journal entry you read, the writer carefully chose vocabulary that implied the narrative viewpoint rather than stating it directly. For example, you could write 'when the parrot appeared, my heart skipped a beat', instead of 'I couldn't believe it when the parrot appeared'.

2 Individually, write your section of the journal entry. Remember to refer back to your spider diagram to help you use the **substituting** and **adding** writing strategies to make sure you use different words.

- Before you write a noun or a verb, think about the words you could **add** before or after it to describe it more fully. For example, 'swooped' could be expanded to become 'gracefully swooped'.

- Think about how you can use **substitutes** for words to avoid repetition. For example, use the word 'forest' instead of 'trees'.

- Remember that you can also **substitute** words and phrases with similes to **add** detail. For example, write 'as blue as the sky' instead of 'bright blue'.

Make sure that you apply the spelling strategies that you have learned to any tricky words that you decide to use.

Improving

Choice of vocabulary

1 **Stick to the objectives.** The objectives for this task were to:
- **add** detail to create a vivid picture for the reader
- **substitute** words with synonyms to avoid repetition
- create a sense of excitement and anticipation, giving your viewpoint about the experience
- use similes to help the reader to visualise what you are describing.

a Swap your writing with another member of your group. Read their section and think about how well they have met the objectives listed above. Annotate their writing to show where they have succeeded at each one. Note any places where they could improve, for example, where they could **add** or **substitute** words.

b As a group, discuss the comments and agree what changes to make. Then, read the whole journal entry aloud. Will the reader be able to imagine the event and understand the narrator's thoughts and feelings about it?

Correct spelling

2 a Working individually, look again at your own section of the journal entry to check the spelling. To help you focus on the individual words, read the text backwards word by word. Pick out any spellings that you are unsure of.

b As a group, check the correct spellings of the words each of you has picked out. Work out a spelling strategy to help you to remember the correct spelling of each word.

▶ Reviewing

1   **Think about the effect on the reader**. In your group, discuss the viewpoint you have presented and review how you have shown the growing excitement and anticipation in your journal entry. Draw a graph similar to the one on page 41. For each paragraph that you have written, decide how high the excitement level is and pick out words, phrases and ideas that help to create this feeling.

2   In your learning diary, explain the work you have done in this unit and what you have learned about writing to imagine, explore and entertain. Record your achievements for each of the objectives below and identify which one will be your target next time you write to imagine, explore and entertain.

   - To choose vocabulary effectively to imply the narrator's viewpoint.

   - To be able to **add** and **substitute** vocabulary to create variety and build up a picture for the reader.

   - To be able to use effective similes.

   - To know and use spelling strategies for remembering tricky words.

Sport

Imagine, explore, entertain

When you are writing to imagine, explore and entertain, you need to be aware of the effect of your writing on the reader. To write an entertaining short story, you need to be able to sequence events in an interesting way and think carefully about the impact of the opening and ending on the reader. Thinking about your reader will also help you to decide what details to include. Using humour is one way to make your writing entertaining, but even the punctuation you choose can add to the entertaining impact of your writing. In this unit you will explore how to use these techniques effectively when writing your own short story.

Writing strategies

- think about the effect on the reader
- choose how to plan
- write for a reader

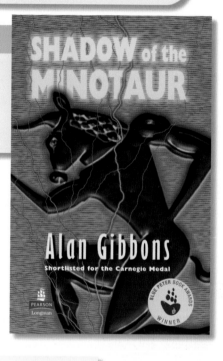

Pre-writing: think about the effect on the reader

The opening of any story is important because it is what hooks the reader and makes them want to continue reading. This opening from the novel *Shadow of the Minotaur* by Alan Gibbons takes the reader directly into the middle of the action.

> The first of the beast's roars almost tore the flesh from his bones. The second, a nerve-splitting bellow that crashed inside his brain, very nearly made him give in before he'd even begun his challenge. He glanced back at the hatch in the door through which he'd just walked and saw the reassuring smile of the dark-eyed girl on the other side. Mustering his own thin smile, he knelt down and picked up the things he'd dropped, a sword with a finely-wrought handle and a ball of strong, thick string.

We don't know why he is there – the writer suggests he has to complete a challenge but we don't know why.

We aren't told who the character is.

We aren't told where he is – it just mentions a 'hatch in the door'.

1 a Choose a story that you have read or a film you have seen that you can remember well. Write down the title and then describe the techniques used in the opening. For example, does the opening:

- speak directly to the reader or viewer?
- start in the middle of the action?
- start with a conversation?
- start with description?
- introduce a flashback?
- shock or surprise the reader or viewer?

Remember that stories and films can use more than one opening technique.

b What is the **effect on the reader** or viewer of the opening you have described? You might want to use some of the following words to help you to explain the effect or choose your own:

- interest • shock • involve • visualise • intrigue

In your dreams

The English department in your school is holding a short story competition on the theme of daydreams.

This notice appears on the noticeboard:

> ### LOOK HERE, ALL YOU BUDDING WRITERS!
>
> This year's short story competition is about daydreams.
>
> We are looking for entertaining pieces of writing about someone who dreams of achieving fame and success ... scoring a winning goal, becoming a celebrity overnight, being the most popular person in the school, getting the better of someone or ...?
>
> You need to think about:
> - what your character daydreams about
> - how these daydreams link with their real life.

Write an entertaining story about someone who daydreams.

Interesting texts

1 a Think about the different ways a writer can make a story 'entertaining' for the reader. Look at the list of techniques below. Working with a partner, can you add any other techniques to this list? Which of the techniques do you think is most important?

- Including realistic and lively dialogue
- Using humour, such as word play
- Choosing words precisely to create entertaining effects
- Creating an interesting story structure to maintain the reader's interest
- Using a range of sentence structures to create interest for the reader
- Creating an appropriate tone of voice for the narrator (e.g. blunt, sarcastic, friendly).

b Look back at the opening of *Shadow of the Minotaur* on page 46. Which of these techniques does its writer use to make it entertaining?

Studying a short story

Read this opening of one pupil's entry for the short story competition:

As I step up to receive my gold medal – MY GOLD MEDAL – the crowd roars wildly. All I can hear are the screams and cheers of English fans; all I can see are beaming faces and Union Jacks flapping frantically. I have come first. I have beaten the world's best and now I am the Olympic champion. I can't believe it. I can hardly see straight – everything is a blur. The National Anthem plays. A medal hangs around my neck. I kiss it and wave to the cameras. It's too much. I must stop myself from breaking down ...

The roar of the TV fills my ears, the cat is sitting on my chest and Mum is tapping my arm.

'What's happened, what's happened?' I mutter.

'The Russians got gold again,' says Mum. 'And you need some beauty sleep, Georgina.'

I stagger up to bed, my brain fluffy with what I'd been dreaming about. Winning gold. Beating everyone.

Organising the ideas

1 In pairs, decide which of the story opening techniques listed on page 47 this writer uses. **Think about the effect on the reader**. How do the techniques chosen help to entertain the reader?

2 The writer also makes the story entertaining by contrasting Georgina's dream with reality. Explain how the writer does this by completing these sentences:

- The noise of the crowd is really …
- Georgina's medal ceremony is actually …
- Rather than having a medal round her neck, she has …

Range of punctuation

3 Re-read this extract from Georgina's daydream. Here, the writer makes the story entertaining by recreating the excitement that the narrator is imagining. Copy and complete the annotated text below, explaining the **effect on the reader** produced by the different punctuation techniques identified.

Pair of dashes to separate out the repeated phrase: the effect is to create a pause and emphasise the importance of the information.

Semi-colon: this links two clauses and emphasises their repeated openings.

Short sentence: this makes the narrator sound surprised and almost speechless.

Dash: this …

Short sentence: this …

Ellipsis: this …

As I step up to receive my gold medal – MY GOLD MEDAL – the crowd roars wildly. All I can hear are the screams and cheers of English fans ; all I can see are beaming faces and Union Jacks flapping frantically. I have come first. I have beaten the world's best and now I am the Olympic champion. I can't believe it. I can hardly see straight – everything is a blur. The National Anthem plays. A medal hangs around my neck. I kiss it and wave to the cameras. It's too much. I must stop myself from breaking down …

That was a laugh. I never beat anyone at anything. I am short, stubby and useless at PE. The only thing I am good at is getting out of PE lessons. Lost PE kit, forged notes, mysterious tummy pains that frighten young male teachers: all these I am brilliant at. But when it comes to doing it, I am about as far from an Olympic gold medal as you can get.

I have lived with it all my life. I laugh it off mostly. But inside this less-than-lithe form, there is an athlete waiting to get out ... Well, I can dream, can't I?

Recently, though, it's got harder because the new girl in our class, little Miss Popularity, has started having a go at me for being so useless at PE. She thinks she's sooooooooo cool.

Take last week. It was the inter-house athletics match. I was lurking in the changing rooms, trying to sneak out as late as possible. As I slunk out on my own, the new girl caught sight of me and started in with the poison, 'Watch out, girls, here comes Miss Blobby – ooh, bet Kelly Holmes is really worried ...' All her mates started sniggering and then as Biggins yelled for us to get ourselves organised, they all pushed past me, jabbing me with their elbows as they went.

I had to do the relay which was OK except, just my luck, I had to take the baton from you know who. As we were all getting ready to go, she was stirring it up with her coven about how I would let the team down and be completely useless.

I tried to ignore it but somewhere inside me I could feel a sense of fury building up. I was completely fed up with her telling me I was useless.

I knew I was useless but it didn't help to have her going on about it all the time. I suddenly felt determined to do the best I could.

Anyway, there I was in position ready to take the baton when the race started. Everyone else from the year was round the edge of the track getting steamed up and yelling and shouting. I was braced in my I-am-ready-to-run-a-marathon position, when, as I waited for my turn, watching that witch streaking towards me, I saw her suddenly double over and stagger towards the edge of the track, groaning pitifully. Suddenly I was jumping up and down, yelling, 'Come on, you've got to get to me, come on ...' Somehow, she managed to reach me and it was like I was suddenly transformed because I seized the baton from her and leapt into my bit of the race like a thing possessed. In fact, I probably wasn't going very fast, but it felt quite fast to me because seeing the Ice Princess fail so dismally had suddenly booted me into action.

And as I ran, I heard something I'd never heard before: other girls shouting for me - yes, for ME - spurring me on, urging me to do my best. And I did. I ran like I had never run before. I really pushed myself - and it felt good. As I got nearer to the end, the cheering got louder and louder till it was like my dream. I could imagine the lights and the crowds and the press and the cameras flashing and I imagined my long, sleek athletic body bounding round the track like a puma. Yeah, I was winning; I was going for gold. The roars filled my ears as I pushed myself towards the last stretch of the race and the finishing line. And then, yes, I was there ... I collapsed, almost sobbing with lack of breath and exhaustion ...

When I looked up, I hadn't won. Our team came second. But I was surrounded by people clapping me and saying well done. They were grinning at me, congratulating me. Even she who must not be named limped up to me and sort of cough-grunted, 'Sorry - it was cramp - you done well.'

I stumbled to my feet and then back to where everyone was standing around and talking ... I hadn't won a medal or anything, I wasn't world champion, but I had been a winner in some kind of way.

Interesting texts

4 You are now going to explore how the writer creates the narrator's tone of voice.

   a Read the following quotations from the story and match each one with the tone of voice it creates. The first one is done for you.

mysterious tummy pains that frighten young male teachers	Exaggerating tone
I am short, stubby and useless at PE.	Matter-of-fact tone
I have lived with it all my life.	Self-critical tone
about as far from an Olympic gold medal as you can get	Humorous tone

   b Find where each of these quotations appears in the text. What **effect** does the tone of voice used have **on the reader**?

5 The writer of this story has chosen vocabulary precisely to describe the main characters.

   a Re-read the paragraph beginning 'Take last week'. What does the choice of the verbs 'lurking' and 'slunk' suggest about the narrator? What is the **effect on the reader**? Can you find any verbs used later in the story that suggest a different image of the narrator?

   b In the paragraph beginning 'I had to do the relay ...', what does 'she was stirring it up with her coven' suggest about the new girl? Can you find any other words and phrases in the story which link with the image of a 'coven'?

Range of punctuation

6 Re-read the paragraph beginning 'And as I ran ...'. How is this description of the race similar to the race in the narrator's daydream at the beginning of the story? Are there any differences? Think about:

   • the length of the sentences
   • the use of punctuation (dashes, semi-colons and ellipsis)
   • the techniques used to entertain the reader.

Organising the ideas

Now read the final paragraph of the story.

> Of course dreams don't come true. Life's not like that. I now realise that that was the moment when my troubles really started ...

7 Why do you think the writer has chosen to end the story in this way? Think about how it links back to the opening paragraph.

8 In a small group, discuss other possible ways the story could have ended.

Planning to write

Organising the ideas

1 a In pairs, you are going to rewrite the climax of this story using the techniques you have studied. **Choose how to plan.** With your partner, discuss what will happen in the climax of your story, noting down your ideas about the following:

- the key moments in the race
- how the people watching behave
- how the narrator feels.

b Remember that you are **writing for a reader**. Think about words you could choose to help them feel involved in your story and add these to your plan.

Composing

Range of punctuation and interesting texts

1 With your partner, now draft the climax of your story. As you write, **think about the effect on the reader**. Remember to pay attention to the sentence structures and punctuation you are using. Remind yourself of the range of techniques used by the writer of the short story you have studied and how to use them: short sentences, semi-colons, dashes and ellipsis.

2 You also need to focus on making the writing entertaining using the techniques you have studied. Think about:

- giving precise descriptive details to help the reader picture the events
- using humour to create a different tone of voice, e.g. a sarcastic tone
- using a mixture of formal and informal language to create a realistic voice for your narrator, if this is appropriate.

▶ Reviewing

1 With your partner, join up with another pair. In your group, compare the way you have used the sentence length and punctuation techniques in the climaxes to the stories you have written. Discuss the **effect on the reader** each piece of writing has created.

2 a As a group, identify the techniques you have used to make your writing entertaining.

b Individually, write down two things that you need to try to improve next time.

LW Task 2 — I didn't think I could do it but …

A publisher is putting together an anthology of writing by young people and for young people about facing up to challenges and overcoming difficulties.

Here is the information the publisher has provided about the anthology:

We are looking for short stories based on real experiences of challenges or difficulties written in a vivid, honest way that will capture the interest and imagination of the reader.

It doesn't have to be a dramatic event – it could be overcoming your worries about something ordinary like starting school or taking part in a sporting event, or anything that for you was a challenge …

Think about
- your thoughts beforehand
- what actually happened
- your feelings afterwards.

Make the reader share the experience!

Write an entertaining short story about facing up to and overcoming a challenge or difficulty.

Planning to write

Organising the ideas

1   **Choose how to plan.** You need to plan the details of the event you are going to write about, the structure of your writing and the features that will make it interesting to the reader.

    a   Start by planning your ideas for the content. Look carefully at what the publisher wants and decide what headings to use in your plan. Look back at the plan you made for the last task to help you.

    b   **Write for a reader.** To make your story entertaining, use the flashback technique used in the opening of the short story you have studied. Make a list of the events of your story in order of time and identify which later part would make a suitable opening. Copy and complete the flowchart below to help you to plan the structure of your story.

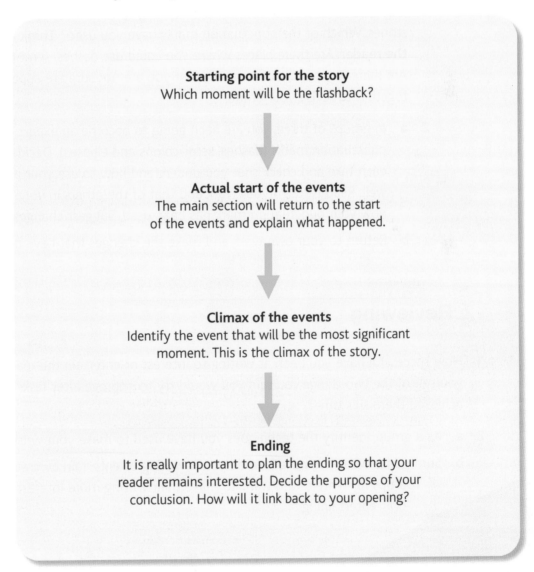

Starting point for the story
Which moment will be the flashback?

Actual start of the events
The main section will return to the start
of the events and explain what happened.

Climax of the events
Identify the event that will be the most significant
moment. This is the climax of the story.

Ending
It is really important to plan the ending so that your
reader remains interested. Decide the purpose of your
conclusion. How will it link back to your opening?

    c   Check that you have created an interesting sequence of events. Identify the features you need to include in your story and the techniques you need to use to do this.

Composing

Interesting texts

1 **Think about the effect on the reader**. Before you start to write, make a list of ways of making your writing entertaining for the reader and refer to this list as you write.

2 Draft your story, making sure that you follow the structure set out in your plan. Start by deciding which opening paragraph technique you are going to use. Look back to the list on page 47 to remind yourself of these. Refer to your flowchart as you draft your story to make sure that you include the appropriate features and use the techniques necessary to do so.

Improving

Range of punctuation

1 In groups of three, look closely at the paragraphs containing the climaxes of your stories. Which of the punctuation marks have you used? **Think about the effect on the reader**. Are there places where you could use dashes, semi-colons or ellipses? Are there any punctuation marks that you are not sure are appropriate? Work together to revise your drafts.

2 **a** In groups of three, you are each going to become an expert on one of the punctuation marks (dashes, semi-colons and ellipses). Decide which one you will each take and check that you understand how to use your punctuation mark well. Read through your work and that of the others in your group, focusing on how your punctuation mark has been used. Suggest changes that could be made.

b Return to your own work and make the changes that have been suggested.

Reviewing

1 How successful have you been at writing to interest or entertain the reader? Remind yourself of the two things you said you would try to improve after Task 1. Have you achieved them this time?

2 **a** As a group, identify the techniques you have used to make your writing entertaining.

b Summarise what you have learned about writing to entertain by creating a poster of top tips for writers who want to make their writing more interesting and entertaining.

The world of work

Persuade, argue, advise

In our fast-moving world, different types of writing have to compete for readers' attention with many other distractions. This is especially true of advertisements as not many people buy newspapers or magazines to read the adverts! This means that space and time are vitally important in advertising. Writers have to make every word count to persuade people to buy a product or to do something. In this unit you will be exploring how to persuade people by using language concisely and precisely for maximum effect. At the same time you will look at ways of increasing your vocabulary and improving your spelling.

Writing strategies

- substituting
- use writers' techniques
- deleting
- adding
- changing

Pre-writing: substituting and adding

1   Working in pairs, use a thesaurus and a dictionary to come up with some more exciting **substitutes** for the underlined adjectives in the following sentences:

- The fairground ride is <u>exciting</u>.
- It is an <u>amusing</u> film.
- These cakes taste really <u>nice</u>.
- You can now buy this incredibly <u>luxurious</u> jacket.

When you put words in front of a noun to describe it, it is called 'pre-modification' because you are modifying (adding to) the noun. Adding extra detail after the noun is called 'post-modification'. Pre-modification is often used in advertising as a way of adding detail in a more concise way than post-modification for maximum effect:

- Pre-modification: the zingy taste
- Post-modification: the taste that is zingy

2 Now choose an item from your pencil case. Write a sentence about it which would persuade someone else to buy it. Try to build lists of adjectives to put in front of the item's name and add descriptions after the noun to give extra detail and appeal. Look at the following example:

> This elegant, crisply sharpened, silver-coloured, unique and fascinating pencil, which is hand-crafted from the finest trees in the ancient forests of northern Europe, can be yours for ten pence.

You'll get points for the lengthiest and most persuasive sentences so remember to use a thesaurus to come up with interesting words and a dictionary to check meaning and ensure the words chosen are appropriate.

Selling school subjects

Your school has decided to make all subjects optional and allow pupils to choose the subjects they study. A subject will only be taught if enough pupils choose it. Not many pupils have chosen your favourite subject so far, so teachers have decided to produce an advertisement persuading pupils to decide to study it. The advertisement will be placed on the school website alongside adverts for other subjects that will be read by pupils and their parents.

You have been asked to write the text for the advertisement and have been given the following writing brief:

- There is limited space and a set format for all advertisements. The text can have no more than three paragraphs and should be between 150 and 250 words long.
- Information about the topics and skills covered in the subject has to be included.
- The advertisement should emphasise that the subject is interesting and enjoyable.
- You should show how the subject would be valuable in life outside school.

Write the text for the advertisement for your favourite school subject.

Studying an advertisement

The English department has produced the following advertisement promoting their subject.

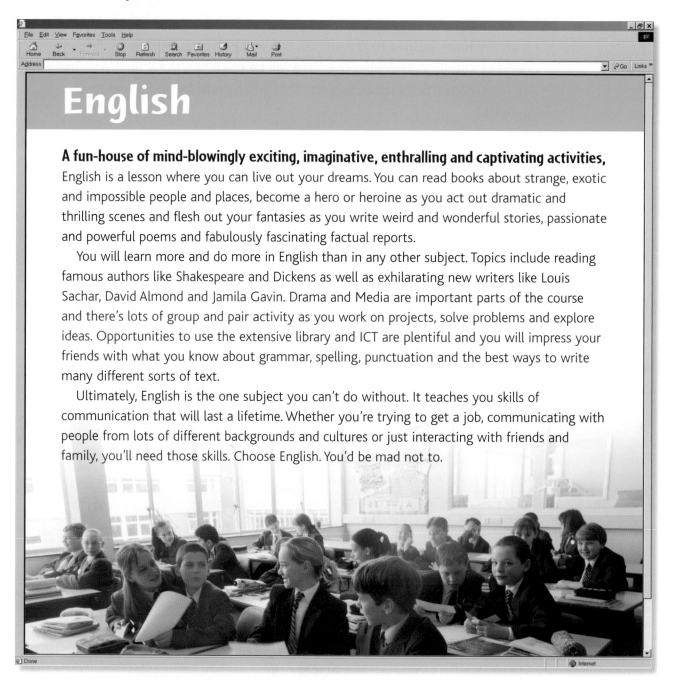

Choice of vocabulary

1   Working in a pair, look at the brief given in the task on page 59 and list the key points from it. Now re-read the text of the advertisement for English.

   a   What are the main ideas in each paragraph?

   b   Have all the key points from the brief been met? Are there any instances where you think they haven't been met or could be improved?

2   The table opposite contains a list of **writers' techniques** that can be used to create a persuasive effect. Copy out and complete the table by identifying where these techniques are used to help persuade the reader in the advertisement for English, giving examples from the text and explaining the effect of these on the reader.

Technique	Example	Persuasive effect
Using words with positive connotations	'A fun-house'	
Pre-modifying nouns		To add in descriptive detail concisely for maximum impact on the reader
Post-modifying nouns		
Using lists of qualities		
Using alliteration and other sound patterns		
Using similes and metaphors		
Using contrast		
Using repetition		
Using exaggeration		

Composing

Choice of vocabulary

1   Decide which of the **writers' techniques** used in the English advertisement had the most impact and include these in your advert. You could pick out any words or patterns of words that were especially effective and use these in your own text.

2   Write the text of an advertisement for your favourite subject. Ensure that you cover the key points from the brief on page 59 in your text.

Improving

Choice of vocabulary

1   Re-read the text of your advertisement. Do you think you have included enough detail? Remember, one way of **adding** detail without adding extra sentences is to **change** existing sentences. You can pre-modify nouns to add extra detail concisely or post-modify to add further information.

2   Experiment by rewriting some of the sentences in your text. **Change** any post-modified nouns to pre-modified nouns. What effect does this have? What happens if you change pre-modified nouns to post-modified nouns? Retain any changes which you think improve the persuasiveness of your text.

▶ Reviewing

1   How effective will your advert be at persuading pupils to study your favourite subject? Which **techniques** would you like to improve on next time you write to persuade?

Task 2 Delivering the right copy

There is a shortage of people to deliver newspapers in your area and your local newsagent has asked you to produce a promotional flyer to advertise the job of newspaper delivery boy or girl.

The points they want you to include in the flyer are:

- The work is paid at £5.00 per hour and involves 8 hours per week.
- Delivery boys or girls will only be asked to deliver to houses within two miles of their own home.
- Benefits of the job include plenty of exercise and fresh air.
- The newsagent and the customers are friendly and appreciative.
- It is a responsible job for somebody who is mature and trustworthy.

The flyer will be sent to homes in the area and needs to have an impact so that the right people read it.

Write the text for the promotional flyer persuading 13–16-year-olds that a job as a newspaper delivery boy or girl is for them.

Planning to write

Choice of vocabulary

1 Working in pairs, look carefully at the brief given in the task and create an outline plan for the flyer.

   a Decide how many paragraphs to use and use bullet points to show what the topic of each is to be.

   b Add notes on each bullet, jotting down the points you wish to make and details of any **writers' techniques** you are going to use.

2 **a** Look again at the brief and pick out the important and appealing aspects of the job. List the words the newsagent uses to describe the job and then look these up in your thesaurus. Are there better words you could use instead? Add these words to the appropriate paragraphs of your plan.

   b In advertisements, writers often try to anticipate and counter negative responses. What aspects of the job might young people think are unappealing? What could you include in your text to persuade people to feel differently about these aspects? Add notes on how you could do this to your plan.

Composing

Choice of vocabulary

1 Start to draft the text for the flyer. Draft sentences for each paragraph. These can be short to start with but you should then begin **adding** detail by pre- or post-modifying the phrases to build persuasive detail into your descriptions.

2 Try out different words from a thesaurus, **substituting** them until you find the ones that sound best and communicate the key points you wish to make.

3 Look back at the table you completed on page 61. Think about **using writers' techniques** for maximum persuasive effect.

Improving

Choice of vocabulary

1 When you have completed your draft, check that it meets the demands of the brief. Then read it aloud to hear how it sounds and make any **changes** that you think are needed by **adding** to, **deleting** or **substituting** the words or phrases you think could be improved.

Correct spelling

2 Swap your writing with a partner. Proof-read the text carefully and mark on it in pencil any queries you have about the choice of words used as well as any spellings your partner needs to check. When your writing is returned, take note of the comments and check the queries by using a dictionary, spellchecker or thesaurus. Make a note of any spellings you need to correct and record the correct spellings in a spelling journal.

▶ Reviewing

1 Working in a small group, in turn read your final versions aloud. Ask for comments and suggestions and make notes about these.

a What positive features of your text were picked out and commented on? Make a note of these.

b What suggestions for improvements were made? Think about these and make a note of the one you thought was the most important.

2 a What did you think was the best part of your text? Write a brief paragraph at the end of your text explaining your view.

b What would you want to improve next time you write this type of text?

Discoveries

Inform, explain, describe

When you are writing to inform, explain and describe, you need to make sure the reader takes in the information that you want them to. In this unit you will explore ways of constructing sentences so that when you describe, you will help the reader to 'see' what you want them to see. By changing the structure of a sentence a writer can determine how the reader will respond to their writing, for example, by placing something at the end of a sentence it can become a climax. You will also explore other techniques that will help to create a vivid picture and an effective mood in your own descriptive writing.

Writing strategies

- write for a reader
- think about the effect on the reader
- adding
- rehearse sentences in your head
- use writers' techniques

Pre-writing: write for a reader

There are many ways to write the same words to make a sentence. The words at the beginning of a sentence can help to direct the imagination of the reader. Think about the difference between these two sentences:

Sentence 1 *There were several yachts in the harbour.*
Sentence 2 *In the harbour, there were several yachts.*

They mean the same thing, but in the first example, the reader thinks about the yachts and then the harbour. In the second example, the reader thinks about the harbour and then the yachts. The focus is changed by putting the word 'in' at the beginning, which helps us imagine *where* the yachts are.

Words like 'in' are prepositions: words telling us *where* a noun is.

1 Working in pairs, think of as many prepositions as you can. Try writing a few descriptive sentences of your own, putting the preposition at the beginning and remembering to include the comma.

2 With your partner, discuss what the effect on the focus and meaning of each of your sentences would be if you were to write it so that the preposition is in the middle, not at the beginning.

The land of the free

A good description can help readers imagine a scene by creating a picture in words. The following example describes the land Christopher Columbus first saw when he reached the Caribbean in 1492.

> On the edge of the horizon, the thick clot of shadows revealed itself to be a forest. The lush greens of this forest, though, were nothing like the colours of my homeland. Some trees stretched for a way above the others, towering over them. As we grew closer, I could see the vegetation was busy with bird life.

Your task is to add to this description of the setting. You can use this passage as the beginning, middle or ending of your description.

The purpose of the writing is to describe to the reader the setting that Columbus saw. Before you begin to read the model text, working with a partner, discuss what stylistic features you would expect to find in a piece of descriptive writing. For example, you might expect there to be lots of adjectives to add detail. Share your ideas with the rest of the class and make a list of all the features that people expect to see.

Studying a description

1 Now read the first paragraph of this description of what Columbus saw. Are any of the features in your list used here?

> The night had been unbearable: sticky, humid winds wrapped themselves around everyone on the ship, and we got little sleep even though the seas were quiet. I slept badly for different reasons though despairing of ever seeing the longed-for land of the Indies. The men, too, had shown signs of hopelessness; many of them wished they'd never trusted me when I said we should sail into these unexplored Western oceans. Perhaps they were right. Was I really so wrong?

Choice of vocabulary

2 a Working with a partner, pick out words from the first paragraph that help the reader to imagine the night. What descriptive words does the writer use?

b How do these words show the mood of the people on the ship?

65

3 Now read the rest of the description below.

    a Pick out the descriptive words that help the reader to imagine the scene.

    b Discuss how these words show us the feelings of the writer and help create the mood of the text.

With only a half-hearted effort, I picked up the telescope. The darkness behind was beginning to lift, but the horizon before us was still cloaked in a blanket of shadows. Behind us, the wan skies were specked with lighter blue, highlighting in silver the wake of the ships, marking where we had been as surely as a footprint. I turned my scope back to the oceans ahead. Was it too much to hope that I might see land? It seemed so. Just then, the first rays of the morning sun crept along the ocean in front of me, illuminating a distant, pale object. I looked again. There, in front of us, the darkness clotted thickly. Below it, a swathe of white. Surely it was sand. Were my eyes deceiving me? In my desperate desire to conjure the mystical Indies, was I now hallucinating? I looked once more. The swathe of white was still there, beneath the thick darkness that lay above it.

Soon, the men were awake, each of them leaning over the side of the ship, squinting into the hazy morning light, through which lay our treasure, our prize.

I studied the land as our ships sailed closer still. It had not disappeared, like some mirage of my mind, and in the wan light it became ever more real as the minutes passed and the light grew stronger. On the edge of the horizon, the thick clot of shadows revealed itself to be a forest. The lush greens of this forest, though, were nothing like the colours of my homeland. Some trees stretched for a way above the others, towering over them. As we grew closer, I could see the vegetation was busy with bird life. Thousands of birds flew from place to place, brightly coloured creatures, more splendid than any I had ever seen – greens, reds, yellows – like nothing on earth.

Below the tree-line, a wide band of white sand gave way to rocks, and then to a natural harbour. Here, the water changed from turquoise to deep blue. Perhaps rocks lay underneath the surface, treacherously waiting to attack the ships if we sailed onwards. Perhaps the welcome of this harbour only concealed these rocks, conspiring to destroy us.

We drew closer to the inlet, manoeuvring into the channel, carefully avoiding any rocks which might be lying beneath the surface. Here, the water lay still and clear, the bottom obscured by depth. Closer to the surface, shoals of curious silvery fish swam up to our ships, slipping in and out between them.

I gave the order to drop anchor so that we could take the rowboats to the shore. Glad as I was that we had found land, we still needed to find some indication of where we were.

Beneath the rowboats, the fish flitted up to us, darting close and then darting away again, curious yet apprehensive.

On the white coral banks on the sea bed, some fish hunted and searched for food: fish the size of a dinner plate, blues and purples; tiny fish, striped in white and yellow, lustrous as gold dust. Around me, the excitement of my men was contagious: they looked, pointed and talked wildly about everything they saw in front of them.

Gradually, coral gave way to sand; the larger fish grew fewer and further between, until only the tiniest remained. Then, the sand grew finer as the rowing boats reached the shore. We were here – finally – in a marvellous land that held such promise and such potential …

4 Where does the mood begin to change in this description? Look back at the words you picked out from the text and explain how the writer shows this change.

5 Re-read the paragraph beginning 'We drew closer to the inlet …' and look at the way the writer has described the fish.

   a Pick out examples of the way the writer has used strings of adjectives in the expanded noun phrases to make the description more detailed.

   b Think about the water in the second sentence of this paragraph. What adjectives could you use before 'water' to describe it? Try to create a string with two adjectives together.

   c How do these strings of adjectives help to make the noun phrases clearer to the reader?

6 Now re-read the paragraph beginning 'On the white coral banks …'.

   a Pick out the similes the writer has used to describe the fish. What **effect on the reader** do you think the writer was trying to create by using these similes?

   b What other similes could you use to describe the colour, size or movement of the fish? For example, what words could you use to make the fish seem fast, colourful or curious?

Using different types of sentences

7 In places in the description, the writer has used a colon to help introduce an explanation.

   a Re-read the whole text and pick out two examples where the writer has done this. What are they explaining?

   b Why do you think the writer wanted to make this clearer for the reader?

8 Look at the first two paragraphs, from 'The night had been unbearable …', where the writer has included several questions. Why do you think there are questions at this point? What is the writer trying to show?

9 The writer has also used prepositions in the description. Prepositions like 'above', 'beneath' and 'below' help the reader to locate where things are.

   a Identify all the sentences that start with a preposition.

   b Then pick out some other prepositions used in the rest of the passage. What does the writer help the reader to focus on by putting the preposition within the sentence?

   c Rewrite the following sentence so that the preposition is in the middle of the sentence.

   On the edge of the horizon, the thick clot of shadows revealed itself to be a forest.

   With a partner, discuss how this changes the focus of the sentence. What effect do you think the writer wanted to create? Experiment with moving the preposition in other sentences from the description.

Planning to write

Choice of vocabulary

1 You are going to write an additional paragraph to add to the description you have read of what Columbus saw, remembering to **write for a reader**.

   a What other sights, smells or sounds might Columbus have experienced when he first reached the Caribbean? Create a spider diagram of details that you could describe in your additional paragraph.

   b **Add** some adjectives to expand any nouns listed with more detail. Then, note down prepositions that you could use. You could put prepositions around your noun phrases to prompt your thinking, as in the following example.

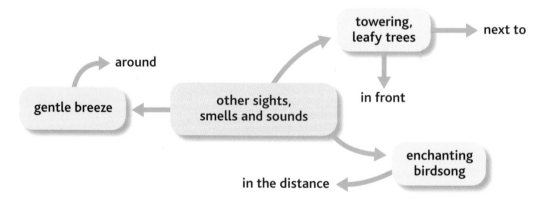

2 a Now put the plan into a sequence. You could write separate ideas on cards and move them around to help you decide on the order you think your ideas should go in.

   b **Add** some temporal connectives to help your reader understand that time is still moving and to organise your writing sequentially. Choose from the following or think of your own: 'at first ...', 'then ...', 'moments later ...', 'just then ...', 'finally ...'.

   c Think about how you could order the prepositions so that they follow on from each other, for example, 'In front of ...', 'Behind ...', 'Below this ...'. This will help the reader's eye to follow your own around the scene and will link the paragraph together, creating cohesion within the text.

Composing

Using different types of sentences

1   Now start to draft your description. As you write, try to keep a balance of longer and shorter sentences. **Rehearse sentences in your head**. Think about where you would like your reader to speed up, or where you would like to emphasise something in your description to make it more noticeable.

2   You will also need to think about the way you start your sentences. Remember to use a variety of sentence structures.

Improving

Choice of vocabulary

1   Look back over your writing and **think about the effect on the reader**. Identify some of the nouns you have used when writing about sights, sounds and smells. Check that you have added the strings of adjectives from your plan to create noun phrases, and **add** more if you feel you need to.

2   Swap your draft with a partner. Ask them to underline three places where more interesting vocabulary could have been used. Work together to think of alternative words or phrases and amend your drafts.

▶ Reviewing

1   **Use writers' techniques**. Remind yourself of the techniques you explored when studying the description on page 66.

   a   Re-read your description. Highlight where you have used similes and strings of adjectives.

   b   Swap your writing with a partner. Ask them to annotate your highlighted sections and comment on the effectiveness of the techniques you have used. Then they should note down any other techniques you have used. Refer back to the list you made on page 65 of features that you expected to see in descriptive writing.

   c   Now your partner should underline one or two sentences that they feel could be better and offer one or two suggestions for improvement.

The last unexplored continent

Early in the twentieth century, Captain Scott and his ship, the *Discovery*, embarked on an expedition to reach the South Pole. It was a dangerous and difficult journey and they were the first British explorers to attempt it.

Here is a fragment of a description of what they saw:

> *Immediately in front of us, the ice stretched out as far as we could see. Between the horizon and us, snow twisted into whirlwinds, swirling and spinning in tiny spirals across the icy landscape. The wind picked up each fragile snow crystal and filled it with life, carrying it in a frenzied dance.*

Write a description of the icy world Scott explored. You can use the passage above as a beginning, middle or ending.

You will need to make sure your reader is drawn into your description of the place and gets a clear picture of the scene. What stylistic features will help you to do this? If you want, you can write in the first person as if you are a character in the scene, using 'I', or you can write in the third person, using 'it' and 'there'.

Planning to write

Choice of vocabulary

1 **Write for a reader.** Before you start, refer back to the list you made on page 65 and select the descriptive techniques you plan to use.

   a Note any sights, sounds and smells you would expect to experience. Remember, you don't need to describe very many things as long as you have lots of ways of describing them. For instance, you could describe the wind four or five times, as long as you vary your description throughout.

   b You can plan your writing in a similar way to the plan you used in Task 1 if you found it helpful. Make sure you add lots of prepositions to your plan to help the reader 'look' exactly where you want them to look.

2 Consider adjectives you could use to describe the nouns in your plan. Remember, you can use strings of adjectives with commas to add more than one. For example, 'snow' could become 'ice-cold snow' or it could become 'bright, ice-cold snow'. Try **adding** several adjectives to each of the nouns in your plan. How many adjectives does it seem sensible to add to each one? Is the number always the same or does it depend what words you choose?

3 Ask a partner to check your plan and **add** some descriptive words or ideas that you could use as well as the ones you have chosen.

Composing

Using different types of sentences

1 a **Rehearse sentences in your head.** Write the first paragraph of your description slowly, thinking of each sentence on its own before you commit it to paper.

   b You could use a mini-whiteboard to help you at this stage as you will need to play around with each sentence until it is exactly as you want it. Remember to **add** your adjectives and think about the length of your sentences.

2 Vary the way you begin your sentences, and use prepositions to help the reader imagine where things are.

3 As you write the following paragraphs, you may find you don't need to practise each sentence before you write it, but you will need to write one sentence at a time, and think about it before you write it.

Improving

Choice of vocabulary

1 **Think about the effect on the reader.** Re-read your work and check that you have included everything you wanted to say. If there are a couple of sentences that you are not happy with, rewrite them in the margin, or underneath your writing. Check your work against the list of techniques used in descriptive writing that you made at the start of the unit. Are there any other techniques you could use here?

2 You can then pass your work to a partner to see if they can annotate some of the features you have used in your writing. They can highlight or underline anything they notice that you have done in your own work. Ask them to comment on the effect of the descriptive techniques you have used by making notes in the margin.

▶ Reviewing

1 Note down at the end of your writing all the techniques you have used. If there are any that you or your teacher thought were very effective, make a note of the ones that worked for you.

2 Use this table to help you work out a target for future work on descriptive writing.

Techniques	I am good at	I tried for the first time	I will use next time
Using strings of adjectives to expand nouns			
Using sentences starting with prepositions			
Putting commas in the right place when starting a sentence with a preposition			
Creating 'colour' in writing			
Using similes			
Putting questions in descriptive writing			
Describing a range of sights, smells and sounds			

Rituals

Analyse, review, comment

When writing to analyse, review or comment, you need to inform your reader of the facts as well as your opinions and experiences. In this unit you will explore techniques you can use to do this effectively when writing a letter commenting on customs and rituals, including varying the tone of your writing and using a range of tenses appropriately. You will also practise planning quickly to develop the skills you will need when writing in tests and exams.

Writing strategies

- ask questions
- think about the effect on the reader
- choose how to plan
- use your plan
- loop back
- changing

Pre-writing: ask questions

1 a Writers often ask questions to help them decide what to include in their writing. You are going to be writing about rituals and customs associated with special occasions in this unit. Working in a small group, discuss the different rituals and customs that you know about, sharing your own opinions and experiences. Use the list of questions below as a starting point.

- What rituals and customs happen on birthdays?
- What rituals and customs happen on other special occasions, such as Christmas, New Year's Eve, Bonfire Night, Diwali, Eid Al-Fittr or Hanukkah?
- Which of the customs and rituals that you have discussed do you particularly like or dislike?
- Have your views changed over time? How did you feel about these customs when you were younger?

   b How effective were these questions in generating ideas about rituals and customs? Which questions were the most effective? Discuss the reasons

How do you celebrate?

A class of students from a foreign country has sent letters to your school. Each class has been given a letter to reply to. Your class's letter is from Jan, who has just celebrated his birthday and is interested in the way birthdays are celebrated in Britain. Jan writes:

> *What customs do you have in your family for birthdays? What do your friends do to celebrate? I want to know what you like and don't like about these celebrations.*

Write a letter to Jan commenting on how birthdays are celebrated in Britain and giving your opinions about the different customs.

Before you read a letter replying to Jan, think about:

* Purpose – to comment on how birthdays are celebrated in Britain, giving your personal view about these customs.

* Audience – someone of a similar age to you from another country.

* Structure – a letter, which will need an opening that introduces the subject and an ending that draws the letter to a close. The letter should balance facts with personal experiences and opinions.

* Style – this should be friendly and appropriate for the audience.

Studying a letter

Here is a letter that another member of your class has written in response to Jan's questions.

Dear Jan,

Thank you for your letter. It was good to hear your views – and I hope you enjoyed your birthday celebrations.

You ask about the way we celebrate birthdays in Britain – and what I think of the customs here. Well, the most common custom is to have a special cake called a birthday cake, with candles on it. You have the same number of candles as your age. However, when my dad had his last birthday, we couldn't find enough candles, so we used just the one. Fifty would have brought the fire brigade! When the candles are lit, everyone sings the song 'Happy Birthday to you ...' then the person whose birthday it is blows all the candles out and makes a wish.

When you are young this is an exciting part of your birthday, and you enjoy being the centre of attention (and blowing the candles out!). As you get older, though, it feels embarrassing and you just want it to be over quickly, without your mum taking too many photographs! In my family, my dad always makes a chocolate cake for my birthday, and we usually have a special dinner. I enjoy this, though I sometimes wish that my gran didn't have to come. My mum gets balloons, which are far too childish for me now, but my brother likes them. We usually have presents after tea – it's a long time to wait – but builds up the anticipation!

My older sister is going to be eighteen this year, which is a special birthday. She would like to have a huge party in a hotel, with all her friends, a live band and gallons of champagne. She has already designed her dress. I think Mum and Dad have other ideas, though, involving a disco in the local church hall. We have held a few family celebrations in the hall. My little brother enjoyed his sixth birthday there, because we found it hard to fit half his school into our house. When I am eighteen I'd like to do something completely different to celebrate, something quite unusual, which I would always remember. I'm not sure what it's going to be yet ...

As far as my friends are concerned, birthdays are a good excuse to get together – not so much for parties now, but more to have fun. We sometimes go bowling or swimming which I like, though I am usually the loser when it comes to bowling. Another thing we do is get together for pizza and a video. Often the video doesn't really get watched which is annoying if you want to see it, but we all sit round and eat pizza, talk and laugh. That's probably my personal favourite and what I will do for my birthday next year.

The other thing we always do at school, though the teachers don't like it, is the birthday bumps. The birthday person lies on the floor, people hold on to his/her arms and legs and 'bumps' him/her up and down the same number of times as his/her age – it's fun to do, but not always as much fun to have it done to you!

Look forward to hearing from you soon.

Chris

Using different text types

1 a Jan has never met Chris. What would Jan learn about Chris from his letter? Working with a partner, create a short fact-file about Chris, noting down what the letter reveals about him.

b How is this information revealed in the letter? Think about the following questions:

- Are family gatherings part of Chris's family life? How do you know?

- What details does Chris include that suggest how old he is in relation to his brother and sister?

- What does Chris write that tells us that his brother and sister have a wide circle of friends?

c Details are built up in the letter to provide the reader with information about Chris indirectly. Go back to your fact-file and add any extra information that you found in part **b**. Discuss how you could include information in this way in your own writing.

2 a After the opening, in each paragraph of his letter Chris refers to the facts about a specific ritual or custom and then links this to his own opinions and experiences. Copy and complete the table below. Re-read each paragraph, noting down the ritual or custom being commented on, the facts given about it and the opinions or experiences Chris comments on. For some paragraphs you may not be able to find both an opinion and an experience. Paragraph 2 has been completed for you.

Paragraph	Main topic	Facts	Chris's opinions	Chris's experiences
2	Birthday cakes	They usually have the same number of candles as your age on them. People sing 'Happy Birthday' then you blow out the candles and make a wish.	–	His dad had only one candle for his 50th birthday.
3				
4				
5				
6				

b In pairs, discuss what you notice about the balance of facts, opinions and experiences in Chris's letter.

c For each paragraph, **think about what effect** the balancing of facts with opinions and experiences has **on the reader**.

3 a What tone is Chris trying to create in his letter? Discuss your ideas with a partner. Think about the purpose and audience that he is writing for.

b What techniques does Chris use in his letter to create this tone? For example, he uses contractions like 'I'm' and 'don't'. What is the effect of this? Re-read the letter and pick out examples of other techniques used that help to create the tone of the letter.

c Are there any other techniques that Chris could have used to contribute to the tone he is trying to create? Look back at the letter and identify places where these techniques could have been used.

Range of punctuation

4 The use of punctuation in the letter also helps to create an appropriate tone. In pairs, discuss the following questions:

- Find examples of where Chris uses dashes. Why might he have used these instead of commas or full stops?
- Where does Chris use exclamation marks? What is the **effect on the reader**?
- What does the use of brackets in paragraph three allow Chris to do?
- Why do you think Chris decided to use ellipsis at the end of paragraph four?

5 The letter is mainly written in the present tense, for example, 'You have the same number of candles as your age'. This is because Chris is giving information about the rituals and customs associated with birthdays, and these are events that take place routinely. However, Chris sometimes uses the past tense, the future tense or modal verbs to develop his ideas.

a Copy and complete the annotated version of the fourth paragraph below, explaining why Chris has decided to use the given verb form in each case.

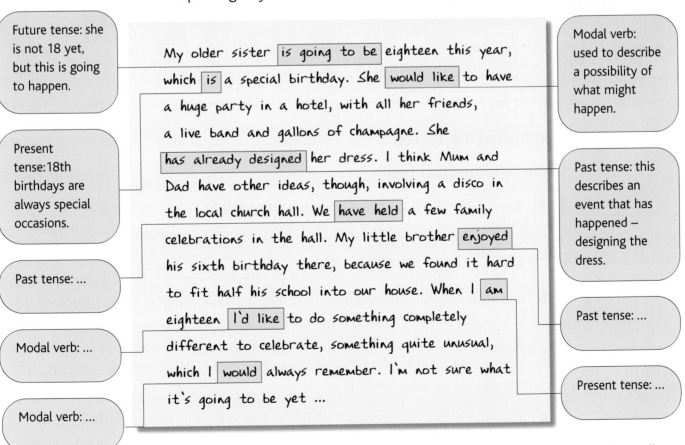

Future tense: she is not 18 yet, but this is going to happen.

Present tense: 18th birthdays are always special occasions.

Past tense: ...

Modal verb: ...

Modal verb: ...

Modal verb: used to describe a possibility of what might happen.

Past tense: this describes an event that has happened – designing the dress.

Past tense: ...

Present tense: ...

My older sister is going to be eighteen this year, which is a special birthday. She would like to have a huge party in a hotel, with all her friends, a live band and gallons of champagne. She has already designed her dress. I think Mum and Dad have other ideas, though, involving a disco in the local church hall. We have held a few family celebrations in the hall. My little brother enjoyed his sixth birthday there, because we found it hard to fit half his school into our house. When I am eighteen I'd like to do something completely different to celebrate, something quite unusual, which I would always remember. I'm not sure what it's going to be yet ...

b Note down what you have learned about using different verb forms. What will you need to remember to help you manage tenses when you write your own letter?

Planning to write

Using different text types

1 a You are now going to plan and write a paragraph to add to the letter to Jan, using your own opinions and experiences about another custom associated with birthdays. In pairs, choose one of the ideas about birthdays that you discussed in the pre-writing task on page 73 that you would like to write about.

   b It is often helpful to be able to plan quickly, to leave you as much writing time as possible, and you need to remember this when you **choose how to plan**. With your partner, spend three minutes creating a plan for your paragraph that includes the main topic, facts about it and two opinions and experiences that you can use to develop the topic.

   c In a small group, discuss what different planning formats you used. How effective was each one? Did you all manage to create a helpful plan within the time limit? Are there any other techniques you could have used that might have been more effective?

Composing

Using different text types and range of punctuation

1 a With your partner, **use your plan** to help you to draft this additional paragraph to add to Chris's letter to Jan. Before you write, think about:

- balancing facts with opinions or experiences when commenting on a custom
- managing tenses effectively to refer to the past and the future
- using modal verbs to show that something might happen
- using a range of punctuation appropriate for the task.

b As you are writing your paragraph, **loop back** to re-read what you have written, checking that you are using the techniques listed above.

2 When you have finished writing your paragraph, read it aloud. What will be the **effect on the reader** of the tone of your writing? Does it match the tone of the rest of Chris's letter? Make any **changes** that you feel are necessary.

▶ Reviewing

1 a Look back at Jan's questions in the letter your class was asked to reply to (page 74). In a small group, read each other's paragraphs. How does what each pair has written help to answer Jan's questions?

b Read each other's paragraphs again. Think about the tone created and what the **effect on the reader** will be. What techniques have been used to achieve this tone? Which were the most successful? Which could they try to improve next time they write a letter commenting on a topic?

Reward review

Your headteacher wants to know what pupils think of the reward system in your school. In a note to all pupils she has asked them to send her letters commenting on the system of rewards.

> We are reviewing the system of rewards in the school – the range of ways we recognise good effort, good work and good behaviour.
>
> What do you think of the customs we have built up? How effective do you think they are? Are there any more effective rewards that we could introduce?

Write a letter to the headteacher giving your comments on the reward system in your school and any ways this could be improved.

As in Task 1, you are being asked to write a letter commenting on particular customs, but this time the audience is your headteacher. How will this affect the structure and style you will need to use for your response?

Planning to write

Using different text types

1 a Read the request from the headteacher carefully. Before you start to plan, **ask questions** to help you decide what to include in your letter.

b **Choose how to plan**. The headteacher has asked people to get their comments to her as soon as possible, so you need to plan quickly. Look back at the plan you created for the paragraph you wrote in Task 1. Can you think of any ways to improve on this planning method for this task?

c Use the responses to your questions to decide what will be the main topic for each of the paragraphs in your letter. How will you organise your plan so that you know what the content of each paragraph will be?

d Create a plan for your letter. Include the facts you will mention in each paragraph and notes on the opinions and experiences you will include to develop these points. Remember that you are writing a letter so you will also need to think about an appropriate opening and ending.

Composing

Range of punctuation

1 Your letter to the headteacher should mainly be written in the present tense because you are commenting on rewards that are used routinely. Before you begin to write, identify in your plan any places where you will need to shift from the present tense to use the past tense, future tense or modal verbs. For example:

- to write about a personal experience of receiving a reward, you would need to use the past tense, e.g. 'I was given a book token when I ...'
- to express an opinion about the possibility of introducing a different reward, you could use modal verbs, e.g. 'Pupils would like to be rewarded more often ...'
- to describe the effect that different rewards will have on pupils, you should use the future tense, e.g. 'They will learn that ...'.

Using different text types

2 Draft your letter, **using your plan** to help you to structure it. Before you begin to write each paragraph, think about how you are going to balance the facts about each form of reward with your own opinions and experiences. As you draft your letter, keep **looping back** on what you have written to check that you are achieving this balance.

Improving

Using different text types

1 **a** You are going to send the letter that you have written to your headteacher. Think about the **effect on the reader**. What tone do you think is appropriate for this audience? Which of the techniques that you identified in the letter on page 75 do you think will be appropriate for this letter?

  b Re-read the draft of your letter and pick out any words or phrases that do not create the right tone for a letter to your headteacher. Try to think of other ways that you could express the same ideas using more appropriate language. For example, if you had written 'You'll never guess what happened!', you could **change** this to 'This had a very unexpected effect.'

▶ Reviewing

1 **a** In small groups, think about the techniques you have learned about in this unit and discuss your strengths and weaknesses in each one:

- balancing facts with opinions and experiences
- managing shifts between tenses of verbs
- creating an appropriate tone for your audience
- using a range of punctuation to create an effect on the reader
- planning quickly and effectively.

  b Individually, set yourself two personal targets that you will try to achieve next time you write to comment on a topic. Write these at the bottom of your letter.

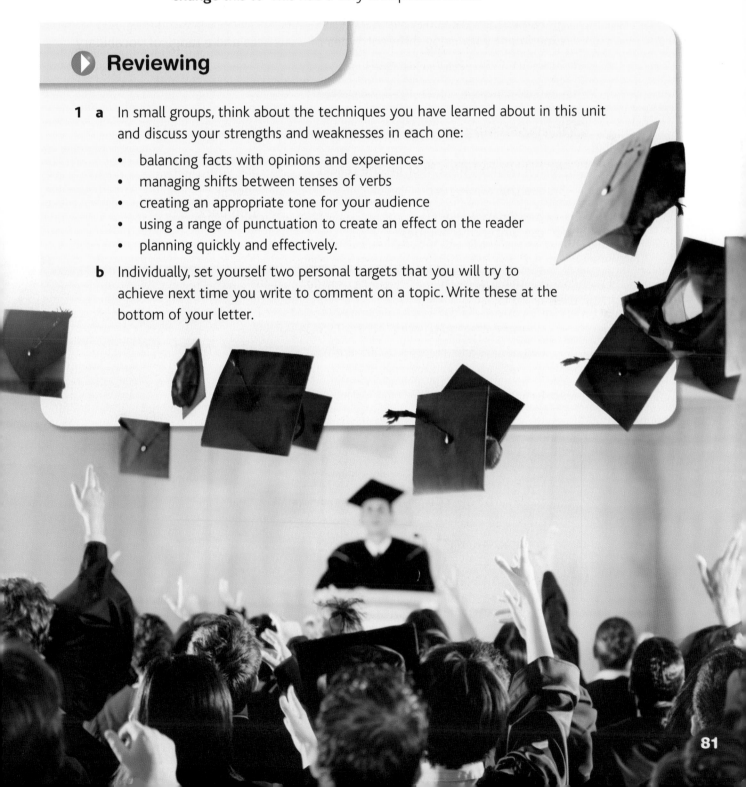

9 Violent Earth

Imagine, explore, entertain

Whether creating a fictional narrative or writing a factual account, when you are writing to imagine, explore and entertain, you need to engage the reader and help your audience to imagine the events you are writing about. Sequencing paragraphs effectively is a vital skill and in this unit you will explore how writers use a variety of sentence openings to create links between paragraphs and to create different effects for the reader. You will also experiment with using different types of sentences and a range of vocabulary to create contrasts in your writing.

Writing strategies

- think about the effect on the reader
- see the whole text
- choose how to plan
- use writers' techniques
- use your plan
- adding
- loop back

Pre-writing: think about the effect on the reader

1 What do you understand by the title 'Violent Earth'? Working with a partner, discuss the ideas and feelings that this title generates. Think of your own experiences of the wild side of nature and discuss any ideas you have gained from television, films or other subjects, such as Geography, about violent natural forces.

2 Many writers have tried to capture the power and awesome beauty of natural forces, such as storms and gales. Working with your partner, read the four short extracts at the bottom of this page. As you read, think about the following questions:

   • What type of writing is the extract taken from?
   • How do you think the writer wants you to feel as a reader?
   • What effects do the choice and order of words have on the reader?

3 Choose the extract that you feel creates the sense of a storm most powerfully. Discuss with your partner which **writers' techniques** have been used to do this. Make a list of the techniques that you could use in your own writing.

> This house has been far out at sea all night,
> The woods crashing through darkness, the booming hills,
> Winds stampeding the fields under the window
> Floundering black astride and blinding wet.
>
> *From* Wind *by Ted Hughes*

> The shutters were bulging as if tired elephants were leaning against them, and Father was trying to tie the fastening with that handkerchief. But to push against this wind was like pushing against rock. The handkerchief, shutters, everything burst: the rain poured in like the sea into a sinking ship, the wind occupied the room, snatching pictures from the wall, sweeping the table bare.
>
> *From* A High Wind in Jamaica *by Thomas Hughes*

> It was wretched weather; stormy and wet, stormy and wet, and mud, mud, mud, deep in all the streets. Day after day, a vast heavy veil had been driving over London from the east, and it drove still. So furious had been the gusts that high buildings in town had had the lead stripped off their roofs.
>
> *From* Great Expectations *by Charles Dickens*

> Their lights poke feebly into the swarming darkness. Spillane can't believe what he sees: massive foam-laced swells rising and falling in the circle of light, some barely missing the belly of the helicopter.
>
> *From* The Perfect Storm *by Sebastian Junger*

Avalanche!

You are a professional author and are working on your new adventure story. You have reached a dramatic moment in your story where your main characters are caught in a violent avalanche on Mount Everest. Here are some research notes that you have made to help you to write the next section of your story.

- Massive snow and ice avalanches are a constant threat on Everest.
- Avalanches can be set off by a number of factors, including temperature change and weight of snow.
- Avalanches can exceed speeds of 100 mph and bury climbing routes.
- Many people have been endangered or killed when their tents have been ripped to shreds by avalanches.

Write the next section of your adventure story, helping the reader to imagine the impact of the avalanche on your characters.

Studying a dramatic narrative

Before you begin to write, you are going to carry out some more research and read an extract from the autobiography of the climber, Brummie Stokes, where he recounts the experience of being caught in an avalanche on Everest.

During the night the wind started to blow up, but sheltered as we were in our tents in the lee of the hill, we knew little about it as we snuggled deep in our bags.

Pulling on my boots inside my tent at 6.15 the next morning, I hear Merv scream a warning, but it came too late. A chunk of ice whistled through the tent in front of my face and the whole world went crazy. The tent, with me inside, was picked up and thrown down the mountainside by what I took at the time to be a big wind. I felt myself being lifted from the ground and rolled around inside the small blue capsule as it was flung down the hill, all my kit tossing and tangling around me as we went. I was screaming with panic, convinced I was going to die without seeing anyone ever again. My mind was racing: I had to do something.

Bouncing off the snow, I felt my shoulder jar as it hit something. I then noticed that a small hole had been made by the ice when it flew through the tent earlier. Pushing my hand into the hole, I ripped a large tear down the side of the bubble I was in, deflated it quickly and was half outside as tons of snow began piling in on top of me. I blacked out.

When I came to, I was swimming for the surface through the suffocating snow. I fought my way clear, knelt up and opened my eyes. What I saw horrified and scared me. Snow and ice blocks were piled up everywhere, bodies lay crumpled and half-buried in the snow, and there were such strong winds blowing that it was almost impossible to scramble to my feet. A loud rumbling noise echoed in my ears together with a high-pitched whine of the wind as it tore savagely at my clothing. I stood up but was immediately bowled over again.

'Oh no!' I thought. 'It's starting again!' Any minute now I expected to be blown away once more, and cried out in anguish, 'God! No! No! Please don't make it now! Please, please don't make it now!'

I was shouting at the wind to stop, like a crazy man. I couldn't understand what was going on, what had happened. Later I learnt that Merv, who had screamed the warning, had been standing outside his tent and had seen a 400 foot frontage of **serac** high on the mountain start to tumble towards us. The crash that followed – after it had fallen free for a thousand feet – shook the whole amphitheatre and triggered off avalanches of powdered snow from both Everest and **Changtse**. The whole lot poured on to us, completely devastating our camp and sweeping it away.

Still numb with fear and shock, I looked up the hill to where Merv was waving and yelling over the wind, 'I'm all right!' But he continued to wave, obviously trying to tell me something. I made out the words: 'Help me! Help me! Bring an axe!'

From Soldiers and Sherpas: A Taste for Adventure *by Brummie Stokes MBE-BEM*

serac: a pinnacle of ice on a glacier
Changtse: a slightly smaller mountain next to Mount Everest

Organising the ideas

1 What kind of atmosphere does the writer try to create in the first paragraph? Copy out and complete the following table, commenting on how the words and phrases used in this paragraph help to create the atmosphere. Pick out another word or phrase that adds to the atmosphere created and explain how it does this.

Word or phrase	Effect
sheltered	
knew little about it	

2 How does the atmosphere change in the second paragraph?

a Look at the sentences at the end of the second paragraph. What do you notice? What **effect** does this have **on the reader**?

b How has the vocabulary changed in this paragraph? Pick out words that suggest the strength of the avalanche and comment on their effect. Pick out contrasting words that suggest the weakness of the narrator.

c With a partner, discuss the way this paragraph is organised. Think about the information included in each sentence and discuss how the way these sentences are ordered in the paragraph helps to build up a sense of fear.

3 Re-read the third paragraph. The writer uses the present participle (the -ing form of the verb) to show the way that one action follows very quickly after the other, using the participle to express the first action, for example:

Pushing my hand into the hole, I ripped a large tear …

a Pick out other examples where the writer uses the present participle form of the verb in this way. For each one, comment on the **effect** created **for the reader**.

b Can you identify the paragraphs which begin with this form of the verb? Why do you think the writer has chosen to open these paragraphs in this way?

c Working with a partner, choose another paragraph from the extract and rewrite the opening sentence so that it begins with the present participle form of the verb. Re-read the paragraph with this new opening sentence and discuss what **effects** this change could have **on the reader**.

4 Re-read the opening paragraph of the extract. Adverbial phrases are used to link ideas in sequence and to provide time links between paragraphs. The extract begins with an adverbial phrase telling the reader when this action begins:

During the night the wind started to blow up …

Now re-read the final paragraph of the extract. The writer begins this paragraph with an adjectival phrase to introduce some information about the subject of the sentence:

Still numb with fear and shock, I looked up the hill …

   a What does the use of this adjectival phrase emphasise about the subject?

   b What **effect** does the placing of the adjectival phrase at the start of the sentence have **on the reader**? How else could this sentence be written?

5 Look back at the extract and **see the whole text**. Creating this image of the whole text in your head will help you to remember the main features. Make notes on what you have learned about the different ways of opening paragraphs. Discuss with a partner what you have found out from this text about using vocabulary and different types of sentences to create contrasting **effects for the reader**. Think about how you could use these techniques in your own writing.

Planning to write

Interesting texts

1 Look back at the task on page 84 and **choose how to plan** the next section of the adventure story. Although you will not be writing the full adventure story, you will need to make very brief notes on what came before this section to help you to plan. Think about how you can use the information you have been given and the ideas from the extract you have read in your own writing.

   a Working with a partner, start to gather your ideas. You could use a spider diagram to record the ideas that you have about:

     • who the main characters are
     • how the avalanche will be set off
     • the effects of the avalanche
     • how the characters will react.

   b Once you have gathered your initial ideas, you could use a flowchart to help you to **see the whole text** and make a note of where you will use different **writers' techniques** to help the reader to imagine the events.

Composing

Organising the ideas

1 **Use your plan** to write the next section of the adventure story. Remember, you will need to use an appropriate style to create a dramatic impact for your audience. **Think about the effect on the reader**.

  a Think about the ways you can help the reader to imagine the beginning of the avalanche. As you write, try to:

    • use vocabulary to create a calm atmosphere in your opening paragraph

    • let your second paragraph explode into action, using vocabulary that contrasts with the opening paragraph

    • vary your paragraph openings, experimenting with the use of the present participle and adverbial or adjectival phrases as sentence openings.

  b Think about the ways you can help the reader to imagine the impact of the avalanche and to believe in the reactions of the characters. As you write, remember to:

    • use a range of words and phrases to add description as well as communicate thoughts and feelings

    • vary your sentence structures to accelerate the pace of your writing as the story moves towards the most dramatic moment.

  c You might want to include some dialogue too. Think about the way the writer of the extract on page 85 has used direct speech and try to use this technique in your own writing.

Improving

Organising the ideas

1 Re-read your first draft to check that the paragraphs of your text link together. Can you follow the sequence of events described? Have you linked your ideas effectively to enable the reader to imagine the events?

2 **See the whole text**. Check that the features and **writers' techniques** that were in your plan are included in the draft. If any are missing, think about the way you could **add** these in to your draft.

▶ Reviewing

1   How well does your completed section of the adventure story help the reader to imagine the impact of the avalanche? Swap your completed draft with a partner. Read their writing carefully and make notes on how effective the text is. Has your partner used:

   • a range of words and phrases to create an appropriate atmosphere and draw out contrasts

   • different types of sentences for effect

   • the present participle (-ing form) of the verb and adjectival phrases at the start of sentences

   • adverbial phrases to sequence ideas and events?

2   Write a brief summary, highlighting the **writers' techniques** your partner has used well and any areas for improvement in the next piece of writing.

   3   Read the summary your partner has written about your own writing. Create a checklist of **techniques** that you want to use or improve on in the next text that you write.

Flood alert

A flood has hit your local area. Here are some photographs you have taken of the flood.

To help raise funds to pay for repair work after the flood, your school has decided to produce and sell a book containing pupils' own accounts of their experiences of the flood. You have been asked to write a 500-word account for inclusion in the book.

In your account, you should write in an imaginative and entertaining way about what happened when the flood began to threaten you, and your thoughts and feelings about the event.

Write the account of your experience of the flood in a way that helps the reader to imagine the event.

Planning to write

Organising the ideas

1 Think about the planning formats that you used for the previous task. Will these help you to plan your account of the flood or do you want to try a different technique? Discuss your ideas with a partner before **choosing how to plan**. You might choose one technique to help you generate your initial ideas and another planning format to organise these.

2 Using your chosen planning format, decide on and then sequence the events that you will include in your account into paragraphs. You could use the photographs to help you with these ideas. Then **add** to each paragraph in your plan the **writers' techniques** and features you want to include. Think about:

- varying your paragraph openings to guide the reader through your account
- using different sentence types and structures for effect
- creating contrasts and links between paragraphs through your use of vocabulary.

Composing

Organising the ideas

1 **Use your plan** to help you focus on the techniques and features you want to include in your account. **Think about the effect on the reader**.

2 As your writing takes shape, **loop back** to check that your account is sequenced effectively. Make sure that you make links between events and the reactions to these.

▶ Reviewing

1 Look back at the checklist that you created at the end of the previous writing task on page 89. Have you met the targets that you set yourself?

2 Working with a partner, compare the section of the adventure story that you wrote in response to Task 1 with your account of the flood. How well do you think you have used a range of **writers' techniques** in each piece of writing? Pick out any similarities or differences between the two texts.

3 What have you learned about writing to imagine, explore and entertain? Write a paragraph summarising your ideas. If you were attempting this type of writing again, which **techniques** would help you produce the most effective writing? Discuss your ideas with your partner.

10 Islands

Inform, explain, describe

When you are writing to inform, explain and describe, you need to give information clearly and precisely, but also in the right amount of detail. The focus of this unit will be how to link your ideas together and create sentences that are constructed so that details can be explained concisely. To help you achieve this, you will explore how, when writing to inform, writers add clauses to their sentences to expand on the main point they are making and link their ideas together logically, concisely and fluently.

Writing strategies

- ask questions
- think about the effect on the reader
- rehearse sentences in your head
- changing
- deleting

Pre-writing: ask questions

Asking questions can help you to generate ideas for the content of your writing.

1 Working in pairs, choose a topic that you would like to inform other members of your class about. For example, this could be an interest you have, something you are studying in another subject, or your views on a topical issue.

2 Now think of some questions that will prompt you to include the information you need when writing about your chosen topic. Remember that you will need to write about the topic in a way that will interest other members of your class. For example, if your topic is fishing, you might ask: what fish can be caught in our local river? This would give you factual information. You might also ask questions that prompt you to express opinions: why do some people go fishing? Here are some question words to help you think of your questions:

- What ...?
- Why ...?
- Where ...?
- Who ...?
- When ...?
- How ...?

3 Now answer your own questions and discuss the answers they produced with a partner. Did the questions prompt the right sort of detail for the content? Can you now think of any better questions?

The island from the sea

A student who is travelling the world is posting entries on her weblog, detailing her travels, and has just visited Surtsey, a volcanic island near Iceland.

Here are some of the photographs the student has taken of the island:

A weblog is an online diary, published on the Internet. This student's weblog gives her family and friends updates about her trip and will also be a record of the trip for the student. Weblogs can include digital pictures as well as text.

The student has decided to write an entry for her weblog giving information about the island.

1 In addition to using questions to help generate ideas for the content of their writing, writers can also **ask questions** to help themselves remember the features of the type of writing they are doing and assess their success when they have finished.

This is the beginning of a list of questions to remind you of the features of writing to inform. What do you know about information texts? Can you add to this list of questions to help you to remember the main features of writing to inform?

Features of writing to inform	Questions
Text level: layout, structure, sequence	• Does my text start with a general opening statement? •
Sentence level: viewpoint, tense, typical sentence structure, linking devices	• Am I writing in the present tense? •
Word level: vocabulary choices, formality	• Does my writing use formal language? •

93

Studying a weblog entry

1 Before starting to write, the student **asked questions** to generate some ideas to include in her weblog. Using the pictures in the task, make a list of possible questions.

2 Now read the weblog entry the student wrote.

 a As you read it, identify where your questions are answered in the text. For example, you might have asked: what are the beaches like? This question is answered in the second and fourth paragraphs.

 b Look at the other information included in the weblog entry. What questions might the student have asked to plan these details? For example, asking 'How was the island created?' might have prompted the sentence that begins, 'This island appeared in 1963 ...'.

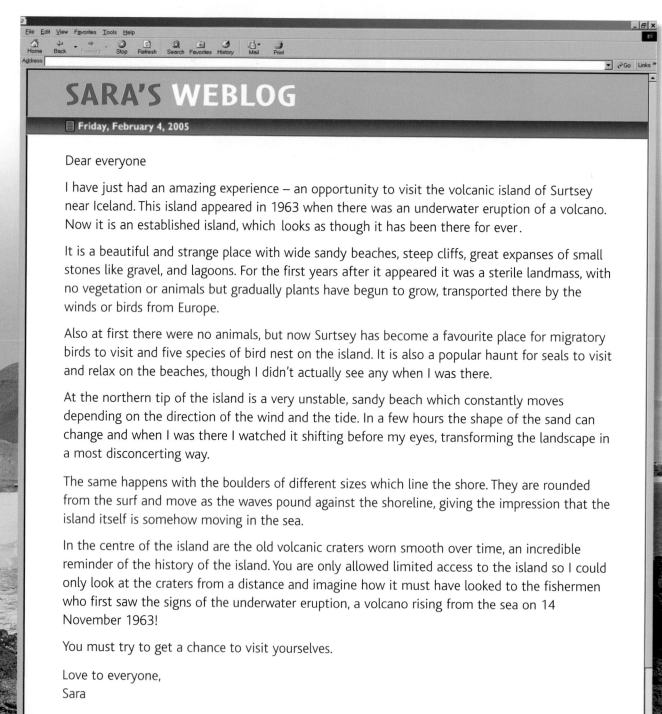

File Edit View Favorites Tools Help

Home Back Forward Stop Refresh Search Favorites History Mail Print

Address   Go | Links »

SARA'S WEBLOG

📄 Friday, February 4, 2005

Dear everyone

I have just had an amazing experience – an opportunity to visit the volcanic island of Surtsey near Iceland. This island appeared in 1963 when there was an underwater eruption of a volcano. Now it is an established island, which looks as though it has been there for ever.

It is a beautiful and strange place with wide sandy beaches, steep cliffs, great expanses of small stones like gravel, and lagoons. For the first years after it appeared it was a sterile landmass, with no vegetation or animals but gradually plants have begun to grow, transported there by the winds or birds from Europe.

Also at first there were no animals, but now Surtsey has become a favourite place for migratory birds to visit and five species of bird nest on the island. It is also a popular haunt for seals to visit and relax on the beaches, though I didn't actually see any when I was there.

At the northern tip of the island is a very unstable, sandy beach which constantly moves depending on the direction of the wind and the tide. In a few hours the shape of the sand can change and when I was there I watched it shifting before my eyes, transforming the landscape in a most disconcerting way.

The same happens with the boulders of different sizes which line the shore. They are rounded from the surf and move as the waves pound against the shoreline, giving the impression that the island itself is somehow moving in the sea.

In the centre of the island are the old volcanic craters worn smooth over time, an incredible reminder of the history of the island. You are only allowed limited access to the island so I could only look at the craters from a distance and imagine how it must have looked to the fishermen who first saw the signs of the underwater eruption, a volcano rising from the sea on 14 November 1963!

You must try to get a chance to visit yourselves.

Love to everyone,
Sara

Done   🌐 Internet

Organising the ideas

3 This weblog entry contains both facts about the island and experiences or opinions specific to the writer's visit. Using different coloured sticky notes, flag facts in one colour and the writer's personal experiences and opinions in another colour.

    a Are there any details that could be in either category?

    b What do you notice about how facts and opinions are organised across the whole text? Why do you think the writer might have organised her ideas in this way?

Using different types of sentences

4 Information texts should convey details clearly and concisely. Writers need to use complex sentences that are constructed so that they focus on particular points, add details and develop the information. Look at this sentence:

| The island appeared in 1963 | when | there was an underwater eruption of a volcano. |

The reader is told when the island was created and that it 'appeared' rather suddenly. Because this information comes first and is written as a main clause, it is made clear that this is the most important fact for the reader to know.

The subordinating conjunction 'when' links the two main parts of the sentence.

The subordinate clause that follows gives information about the cause that led to this effect: a volcano erupting underwater.

    a The way that information is organised in sentences affects the emphasis and can create different **effects on the reader**. Find other ways of writing this sentence. For example, you could break it into more than one sentence or you could **change** the order of the information in the sentence. **Rehearse each sentence in your head** before writing it down.

    b Which version do you think is the most effective? Give a reason for your decision.

5 Writers have to decide how much detail to **add** to nouns and whether to use pre- or post-modification to do this. These decisions will affect the pace and fluency of the writing.

    a Re-read the second paragraph of the weblog and identify where the writer has pre-modified nouns. How has the writer ensured that her use of pre-modification does not disrupt the rhythm of her sentences? For example, think about the amount of detail given about each of the nouns in the second sentence.

    b One way that writers can post-modify nouns is by using relative clauses to **add** details after the noun. Relative clauses allow you to introduce a new idea or piece of information and relate it to information that has already been given. Look at the following sentence from the weblog:

| Now it is an established island, | which | looks as though it has been there for ever. |

The main clause includes the noun, 'island'.

The relative pronoun 'which' links the relative clause to the noun 'island'.

The relative clause expands the main point of the sentence; that the island seems always to have been there.

c Look back at the weblog entry and pick out any other examples where the writer has used a relative clause to expand on the main point of the sentence. Choose one of these and label the sentence to show the noun, the main clause, the relative clause and the relative pronoun.

Correct spelling

6 Word endings are easy to misspell. Look at the following words from the weblog entry:

- different • migratory • experience • incredible

a Working in pairs, discuss the spelling errors you think people often make with each of these words. Why do you think people make these types of error? Hint: try saying the words aloud. Can you recommend a way for people to remember the correct spellings?

b People sometimes confuse the word endings -ary, -ery and -ory, for example, in 'migratory'. With your partner, make a list of words that have any of these endings. Use your list to investigate whether there is a rule that can help you work out which is the correct ending.

Composing

Using different types of sentences

You are going to add a further paragraph to the weblog entry you have read in response to the question: what is the south of the island like? Here are some notes the writer made in answer to this question:

The south of Surtsey:
- a lagoon – azure, warm, healing properties
- rowing boat – fishing net, tarpaulin
- flowers – exotic, dazzling
- dwelling – derelict, tufts of grass on paths
- a hermit used to live here – survived by eating fish and birds, left when tourists started to visit
- during the visit – swam in lagoon, thought about lonely life of the hermit.

1 Take one feature about the south of the island from the notes and write it as a simple sentence. For example, 'The lagoon was warm'.

    a Can you pre-modify any nouns in your sentence? For example, 'The *warm* lagoon'.

    b Practise different ways of developing your sentence:

- using a subordinate clause – for example, '*When you dip your toe in*, you can feel the heat from the warm lagoon ...'

- using a relative clause – for example, 'When you dip your toe in, you can feel the heat from the warm lagoon, *which has healing properties* ...'

- adding any other information into the sentence – for example, 'When you dip your toe in, you can feel the heat from the warm *azure* lagoon, which has *remarkable* healing properties ...'

2 Now complete the rest of the paragraph. **Rehearse sentences in your head** before writing them down to help you to experiment with the structure of the sentence and decide on the most effective version. Think of ways of **changing** the order of your words, clauses or sentences, so that you emphasise the right information. Remember that using a variety of sentence structures will help to create a fluent piece of writing.

Improving

Using different types of sentences

1 Swap your paragraph with a partner. Re-write their paragraph by **deleting** any unnecessary words to make the writing more concise. Then decide whether you need to **change** the order of any words, clauses or sentences so that the reader is made to focus on the most important details. Now compare the two versions of the paragraph and discuss the changes made.

▶ Reviewing

1 Re-read the best version of the paragraph you have written. Copy out and complete this checklist to help you to evaluate how successful you have been.

Have you	✓ ✗	Example
Pre-modified the nouns?		
Used a relative clause?		
Placed a subordinate clause at the beginning of a sentence?		
Placed a subordinate clause at the end of a sentence?		
Placed a subordinate clause in the middle of a sentence?		

Desert island

You are on a round-the-world trip and visit an uninhabited desert island.

Here are the photographs you took of the island:

Write an entry for the weblog you are keeping about your journey,
giving information about the island.

Planning to write

Paragraphs and links

1   Start by **asking questions** to help you gather some ideas for the content of your weblog entry. Remember that your weblog will be read by your family and friends to find out about the places you have visited, as well as being a record of your trip. Carry on the list of questions below:

•   What are the main landmarks on the island?

•

2   Then make notes by answering each of your questions in detail, but remember you don't need to write in sentences at this stage.

3   Now decide on the best order for the information you have. Plan how you will link facts about the island with your opinions and experiences and think about the techniques you could use to do this.

Composing

Using different types of sentences

1   Start to draft the first paragraph of your weblog entry. **Rehearse your sentences in your head** so that you choose the most effective sentence structures to present the information clearly and with the right amount of detail to interest the reader and help them to share in your experiences.

2   Continue in the same way for the remaining paragraphs. Remind yourself of the different sentence structures you could use and try to include all of them in the weblog entry.

Improving

Using different types of sentences

1. Working with a partner, choose one of the paragraphs from your weblog entry and discuss different ways of structuring the sentences. Do the suggestions help to give information more clearly and effectively? Make any **changes** that improve your entry.

Correct spelling

2. Proof-read your entry. Focus in particular on any tricky word endings. Check any that you are unsure of in a dictionary.

▶ Reviewing

1. Look back at the checklist you used when you reviewed your writing in Task 1 on page 98. Identify which sentence structures you have used in your weblog entry. Add another example of each type of sentence from your work.

Aliens and UFOs

Analyse, review, comment

Writing that analyses, reviews and comments sometimes needs to provide its audience with a range of different views and allow the reader to make a balanced judgement. Newspaper reports are one type of analytical writing, but reports are also written by organisations and businesses to look at specific issues and events. They explore all sides of an issue, considering all options and viewpoints. Report writers need to think carefully about how best to organise the views and evidence they need to present, both across the whole text and within each paragraph, and in this unit you will explore the techniques they use to do this.

Writing strategies

- stick to the objectives
- see the whole text
- think about the effect on the reader
- choose how to plan
- use your plan
- loop back

Pre-writing: stick to the objectives

1   In pairs, read the three school reports below. For each report, decide whether it presents just one point of view or a range of strengths and weaknesses in a more balanced way.

ARMITAGE TECHNOLOGY COLLEGE REPORT

HISTORY

Nathan has made disappointing progress in History this year. Not only does he lack attention, but also some homework pieces have not been handed in. As well as taking part more regularly in the group discussions, he would also benefit from improving the way he organises his points.

DESIGN AND TECHNOLOGY

Nathan always tries hard in this subject. As well as having lots of creative ideas for his designs, he can also see how to make them work. In addition, he is able to produce clear diagrams and is improving his ability to write evaluations of his products. He uses equipment sensibly.

TUTOR COMMENTS

Nathan is a pleasant pupil who takes part well in tutorial activities. He is punctual and rarely absent. However, he has been warned on several occasions about the need to wear the correct uniform.

It is clear that he has ability and is generally making steady progress but lack of attention in some subjects is preventing him from achieving his potential. Although the quality of his work in some subjects, like Design and Technology, is good, it is disappointing that he has not made a similar effort elsewhere.

2 Connectives are words that link phrases or sentences together. Balanced reports use connectives both to link ideas and to show a contrast between different points of view.

a Re-read the three reports and pick out the connectives each writer uses. Copy and complete the table below, deciding which category each connective belongs to.

Connectives that link comments from the same point of view	Connectives that contrast points of view
and	but

b Can you think of any other connectives to add to the table? Refer back to this table when you are writing your own report to help you to **stick to the objectives**.

Monster in the lake?

A teenager thinks she has seen a mysterious creature in a lake in your area. The following information is from the local newspaper and a local radio programme:

Terrifying ordeal for teen

Stacey Potter, 14, was frightened out of her wits by seeing what she describes as 'a huge lump' moving in the lake, as she walked home last night. This is the third time a sighting of a strange creature has been reported …

Parents are not allowing their children to go out in the area alone. They have called for a thorough investigation into reports of a strange monster. Expert zoologist, Peter Dock, says it is highly unlikely that a 'huge' creature could be hidden in the lake …

As a member of the local council, you have been asked to present a report on the situation at an emergency council meeting called to evaluate the problem and decide on a response. Your report should give an unbiased account of the situation that will help council members to make a balanced judgement.

Write the report for the council meeting, analysing the different views on the monster and recommending the course of action to take.

Using different text types

1 You have been provided with evidence from three different sources giving different points of view about the existence of a monster.

   a Working in pairs, copy out and complete the table below. Firstly, decide whether each point of view presented seems to support the existence of a monster or not.

   b Then think of a balancing point of view, or counter-argument, for each piece of evidence. The first one has been done for you.

Point of view	For or against the existence of a monster?	Balancing point of view
The expert says it is 'highly unlikely' that there is a 'huge' creature in the lake.	Against	He hasn't ruled it out totally. Perhaps a smaller creature exists?
Stacey said she saw a 'huge lump' moving in the lake.		
Parents won't allow their children to go near the lake alone.		

2 a Think about what you already know about the features of report writing. Remind yourself of this report's audience and purpose and make notes in response to the following questions to help you to think about how you would write it:

   • How formal do you think the report needs to be? What techniques could you use to achieve this?

   • What would be the best way to organise the report?

   • How should the report begin and end?

   • How could you organise the middle section of the report to make sure you present the different views in a balanced way? What techniques could help you to do this?

   b Working in a group of four, share your answers and add any new points to your notes.

Studying a report

Here is a report that another member of the council has written for the meeting.

What did Stacey Potter see?
A report on the supposed sighting of a monster in the lake

Fears have arisen once again about the 'monster in the lake', the local legend which has terrified young people in the area for years.

In this latest incident, Stacey Potter, who is a local 14-year-old, was walking home from Guides when she claims her eye was caught by movement in the lake. When she looked more closely, she saw what she described as 'a huge lump' moving. Stacey's mum and her head of year at school describe Stacey as a sensible girl and not the type to imagine things. Stacey gave a clear account of what she saw, although she was upset, and there is no reason to believe that she is making it up. What then is the explanation?

Susan Brown, a psychologist, says people's eyes do play tricks on them and especially when it is getting dark. It is easy to be mistaken about the size of something or to think that, for example, a shadow or some algae is actually a living creature. That is what could have happened to Stacey. But Stacey says she didn't believe it at first and blinked several times to check what she was seeing. She is absolutely certain about what she saw – so what could it have been?

There have been three previous sightings of something strange in the lake and naturalists from the Natural History Museum were asked to investigate. In the event, no investigation was carried out but a local zoologist, Peter Dock, says it is highly unlikely that any kind of unnatural creature could be living in the lake. This is a reassuring conclusion and if the council agrees with this, it could mean that no further action is needed.

Feelings are running high, however, and local parents are becoming anxious about the safety of their children. They are reluctant to let them out at night and most parents are not allowing their children to go anywhere near the lake. Is this a rational and sensible decision on the part of parents or is it an irrational and hysterical reaction? On the one hand, a local father of three, Jim Donwens, thinks it is right to be cautious: 'It's not as though this is the first time something has been seen in that lake. It wasn't checked out then and noone's bothering to do anything now. What can I do as a responsible parent except keep my children in until I know it's safe?' On the other hand, Mina Ward, whose daughter is a friend of Stacey Potter, is more pragmatic: 'Yes, I do feel anxious but as yet there's no hard evidence that there's anything to be really scared of so I am trying to act normally. I still walk near the lake and so does my daughter.'

What should the council do? Common sense suggests that there is probably nothing to worry about; no monster and no aliens keen to snatch young children. But people are afraid and feelings are running high: the council needs to allay these fears. It must take them seriously and be seen to do so. Experts from the Natural History Museum must be contacted and a thorough investigation carried out. Only then will local people feel safe.

Organising the ideas

1 a Working with a partner, read the report and pick out the points that suggest there is a monster and those that suggest there isn't.

b Place sticky notes labelled 'Monster' and 'No monster' to help you to see where these points are made. What do you notice about the way these points are organised in the report?

c Now draw a flowchart showing the way the points are organised in the report to help you to **see the whole text**. Use the example on the right to start you off.

d Pick out the connectives used in the report to contrast the points of view. Add these to the linking arrows on your flowchart. What type of connectives has the writer used? Why do you think these connectives were chosen? Are there others that could have been used?

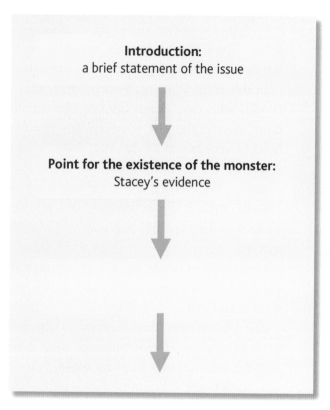

2 Re-read the final paragraph of the report. Explain how each sentence in this paragraph links to information given previously in the report. What **effect** does this have **on the reader**?

Using different text types

3 The writer has used a range of techniques to make the report sound formal. Look at this extract from the report:

Feelings are running high, however, and local parents are becoming anxious about the safety of their children. They are reluctant to let them out at night and most parents are not allowing their children to go anywhere near the lake.

a Rewrite the first sentence to make it sound less formal. To help you, think about how you would say it if you were chatting to a friend. Then compare the two versions of the sentence and identify the things you changed.

b The report is written in the third person, for example 'local parents' and 'They'. Why has the writer chosen not to write in the first person using 'we' or 'I'?

4 Look back at the notes you made on page 104 about the way this report could be written. Which of the features you identified were used in this report? Are there any other features used in this report that you would now want to add to your list?

Planning to write

Organising the ideas

1 Writers create a plan before they write, but we can use 'reverse' planning to look at a finished text and work out what the plan might have looked like. Working with a partner, you are going to create a fishbone plan for the report you have just read. Copy out the fishbone plan below and then add the following information:

- Along the spine of the fishbone plan, label the issue being analysed: 'Is there a monster in the lake?'
- Add notes on the content of the introduction in the head of the plan.
- Along each of the top bones, write the evidence that seems to support the existence of the monster given in the report.
- Along each of the corresponding lower bones, write the balancing viewpoint for this evidence.
- Against each bone, list the points that support that viewpoint.
- Add notes on the content of the conclusion in the tail of the plan.
- Leave one set of bones empty – you will add to this plan later in the unit.

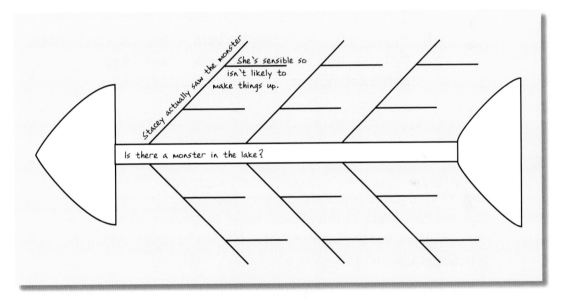

2 It is important when you **choose how to plan** that you make sure the method you choose will help you to organise your ideas as well as to make notes on the content.

   a With a partner, discuss why the fishbone plan is a suitable method for planning an analytical report.

   b Which other planning formats might be suitable for this type of writing?

3   One of the previous sightings of the monster was by a local fisherman who saw movement in the water while he was packing up to go home. You have been asked to write an additional paragraph for the report about this sighting.

   a   With your partner, using the set of bones you left empty on your fishbone plan of the report, make notes on the ways the fisherman's evidence could be used to support views for or against the existence of the monster.

   b   Discuss how to link your points together to present a balanced analysis of the evidence. Refer to the list of connectives you made in the pre-writing task on page 103 and select some suitable ones to add to your fishbone plan.

Composing

Paragraphs and links

1   Before you start to write the additional paragraph on the fisherman's sighting, remind yourself of the key features of report writing. Look back at the report you have read if you need to remind yourself how to use these techniques.

   a   Now write your paragraph. **Use your plan** as you write, making sure you refer to all of your points and choose an appropriate order for them.

   b   As you write, use the **looping back** writing strategy. This will help you make sure that your ideas are logically developed and linked and that you maintain a formal writing style.

 **Reviewing**

1   Join with two other pupils and compare your paragraphs. Work together to find evidence that you have **stuck to the objectives** set for the task. Pick out the connectives used in the paragraphs and highlight any other features of report writing that have been used effectively.

2 Is it worth it?

The government is deciding whether or not to invest a large sum of money in a space project that will try to find out whether there is life on Mars. The following views have been reported in the media:

> Millions of pounds could be wasted on a pointless space project, just to see whether there might be aliens on Mars. This is all while people are waiting for months for operations …

> … It is important that this country keeps up with the space race and that money is invested in the future. Scientific research is very important – people are interested.

You are the head of an independent committee that is discussing the need for the space project. Government ministers have asked you to write a report analysing the different views about the proposed space project. Your report will be used by the government to help them decide whether it is a good idea to invest in the space project.

Write a report for the government, analysing the different views on the proposed space project.

Planning to write

Organising the ideas

1 a Working in pairs, **choose how to plan** and decide on the planning formats you could use to plan an analytical report. Take a different format each and, working on your own, create a plan for the report. Remember that you will need to include:

- points of view in favour of the project
- opposing viewpoints against the project
- supporting evidence to develop these different viewpoints
- the information you will include in your introduction and conclusion.

b Compare your plan with your partner's. Which do you think will be the most useful plan? Why?

c Now discuss how you will organise your report. Where are you going to make the different points and what connectives can you use to link the ideas? Draw a flowchart to help you **see the whole text** and refer to this as you write.

Composing

Paragraphs and links

1 a **Stick to the objectives**. Check that you understand how to achieve the objectives of this task:

- present different points of view in a balanced way
- organise the report to show that you are considering all viewpoints
- use connectives to link the points you make
- use formal language.

b Make a note of any personal objectives you are also trying to achieve. You could write the objectives on the top of your work or on your plan, so they are always visible.

2 As you write, remember to **use your plan**.

a Look at your notes for the introduction and draft your opening paragraph. You need to outline the issue that you are going to discuss and make it clear that this is a balanced report.

b Now present the first point of view about the project and make links to each of the details in your plan. Continue your report according to your plan, ensuring that you cover the different viewpoints in a balanced way.

c As you write, remember to **loop back** to re-read each section as you write it. Focus on expressing each point clearly and check that you are writing in an appropriate style. Looping back will also help you to know when you are ready to move on to the next point.

3 End your report with a conclusion that sets out your recommendations in a balanced way. Re-read the ending of the report on page 105 and think about how you can use some of its techniques in your ending.

Improving

1 Compare your draft report with your plan. Are there any points that you haven't included? Try to find a way of adding these to your draft.

2 a In pairs, swap your reports and use the following marking code to identify where your partner needs to improve their text:

- Circle places where they need a better link between points.
- Draw a star where they need to add more detail.
- Underline places where they need to use more formal expression.

b Ask your partner to explain their marking of your work. Discuss what changes you could make to address these comments.

c Work individually to revise your own report.

▶ Reviewing

1 Review your completed report and compare it to your plan. Working in a group of four, discuss the following questions:

- When you were composing your report, how did the plan help you to decide what content to include and to organise and develop your ideas?
- What planning formats did you use? Were any of these more effective than others?
- What type of plan will you use next time you write an analytical report?

2 How well did you **stick to the objectives**? For each of the objectives for this task (listed on page 110), write a few sentences explaining how you think you have met the objective and include an example from your work for each one.

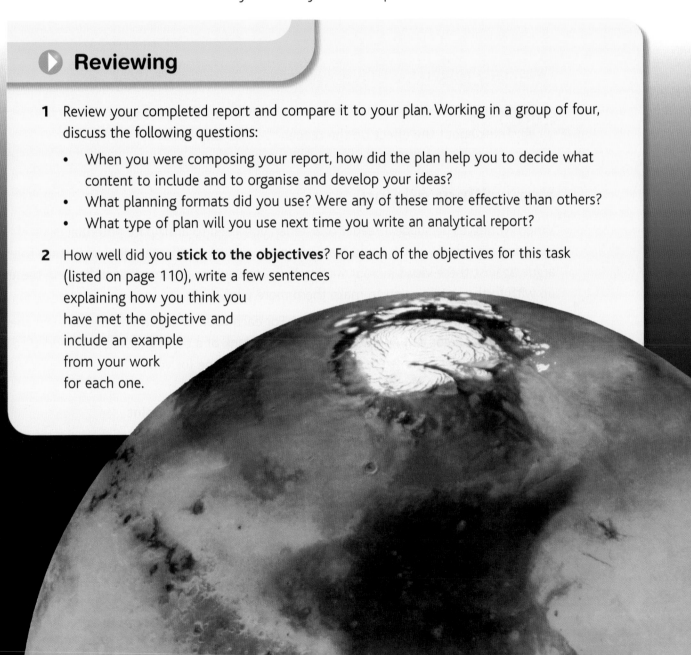

Food, glorious food

Persuade, argue, advise

When you are writing to persuade, argue and advise, it is important to consider what you can do to make your writing have a powerful effect on the audience. In this unit you will write a speech that persuades the listener to share your viewpoint, developing counter-arguments to deal with possible objections. You will explore how to use a range of persuasive techniques and look at how punctuation can be used to help you communicate your meaning effectively.

Writing strategies

- adding
- think about the effect on the reader
- write for a reader
- loop back

Pre-writing: adding

When writing to persuade a reader or listener, you need to anticipate potential opposing arguments which could make your argument less effective. It is important to argue against these views in your writing by using counter-arguments and backing these up with further information to make them more persuasive.

1 **a** Copy and complete the table below. For each counter-argument, decide what the original argument might have been. Then think of a point that could be added to the counter-argument. The first one has been done for you.

Argument	Counter-argument	Added point
Eating excessive amounts of chocolate is bad for you.	That doesn't mean you can't eat your favourite chocolate bar once in a while.	I bet most athletes and other healthy people eat some chocolate.
	It is important for pupils to have a hot meal at lunch time, particularly in the winter.	
	Fast food should not be marketed to young children.	

b In pairs, discuss how a writer could present these arguments and counter-arguments. Select one of the three examples above and discuss how the three elements could be organised into a paragraph. What would the writer have to think about when composing the paragraph?

A little bit of what you fancy ...

A group of students at your school has opened a 'Healthy Hut' at break time, selling only healthy food, in aid of charity. This is what their publicity flyer says:

Healthy Hut

School is full of temptations! No more packed lunches from home. You're free to eat what you want, when you want it. You can pile on the portions in the canteen, eat meals of chips, pizza and ice-cream, and reward yourself with doughnuts and fizzy drinks to fuel yourself for lessons. School is also a time of change, and the stress of getting used to your new school can trigger overeating. You want to be one of the crowd, so it's easy to share your unhealthy food with your new friends. Not surprisingly, you'll pay the price - you'll become a spotty lardy-butt!

Avoid all this — and come to the Healthy Hut!

You don't agree with these views so you have decided to raise money for charity by selling home-made chocolate cakes at break time. You are going to give a speech in assembly to persuade pupils and teachers to forget their diets and buy chocolate cake from you.

Write the speech that you will give at the whole school assembly to persuade pupils and teachers to buy your cakes.

Planning to write

Interesting texts

1 It is important to think carefully about how to make your speech appropriate before you begin to write. Copy and complete the following table to help you remember the key points to bear in mind as you write.

	Information in the task	What this means I need to do
Viewpoint	• You are a pupil at the school. • You are trying to raise money for charity. • You like chocolate and disagree with the Healthy Hut's publicity.	• Use the first person ('I'). • Give the pupil perspective on the issue. • Explain that not all pupils think the same about what should be available to eat in school. • Recognise people in the audience might have different views.
Purpose	• Persuade people to buy chocolate cake rather than healthy food, to support charity.	• Use techniques that persuade, for example … • Give counter-arguments that …
Audience	• Teachers and pupils in the whole school.	• Use language that is …
Content	• Counter the arguments for healthy food. • Tell people that you are supporting a good cause.	• Give information about …

2 Your speech should try to persuade people not to go to the Healthy Hut and so you will need to argue against each of the points made in their publicity flyer.

    a In pairs, re-read the Healthy Hut flyer and pick out the arguments that are given about why people eat unhealthily at school. Create a fishbone plan and add each of these arguments to one of the top bones, for example, 'Pupils kid themselves that they need junk food to give them energy for lessons'.

    b For each argument that you have picked out, think of a way to argue against it (a counter-argument) and add these to the corresponding bottom bones, for example, 'You can't be expected to make it through the day on something as insubstantial as a salad'.

Studying a speech

One of your friends has agreed to help you set up the chocolate cake stall and has written this speech for you to give in assembly.

A little of what you fancy ...

Sick of sad salad? Tired of tasteless tomatoes? Had it with wholemeal? Have we got the answer for you! Spice up your life – come to the Chocolate Chamber. Indulge! Spoil yourself! Taste nectar at the gates of heaven!

Yes, it is true that we need to eat healthily, but the last thing we need in a school day is deprivation. Aren't we deprived enough? Most importantly, to deprive ourselves of the things that our bodies crave is just – wrong. And what's worse is that we are made to feel guilty about the little luxuries in life that can make us feel good. Well, now you can have your cake and eat it – without guilt! Guilt's a most over-rated trip anyway ...

It would be stupid to think that we are all so weak-willed that we 'share our unhealthy food with our new friends' to be 'one of the crowd'. What could be more generous than sharing something that YOU REALLY WANT with your new friends? Well, now you can. And you can do more than just share your favourite food, you can also give generously to our nominated charity – the RSPCA. So – a guilt-free trip!

Where? When? How? The Chocolate Chamber will be open every break time in the canteen next week. Two rules apply. Nothing healthy will pass your lips and all money will be donated to charity. And just remember – a little of what you fancy does you good!

Interesting texts

1 a The purpose of this speech is to persuade pupils and teachers to visit the Chocolate Chamber. To help make the speech persuasive the writer has used the techniques of giving counter-arguments and **adding** further ideas to strengthen the points made. Re-read the following section, which has been annotated to show how these techniques have been used.

> Argument: agrees with basic point in Healthy Hut flyer.

> Counter argument: makes the opposite point that eating healthily doesn't mean we can't also eat the things we want. 'Deprivation' suggests that healthy food doesn't satisfy us.

Yes, it is true that we need to eat healthily, | but | the last thing we need in a school day is deprivation. | Aren't we deprived enough? | Most importantly, to deprive ourselves of the things that our bodies crave is just – wrong.

> Question added: use of the pronoun 'we' encourages the audience to share this viewpoint.

> Added point: this helps to make the speech persuasive, by arguing that not to eat the things we want is actually wrong, even unnatural.

115

b The next paragraph of the speech introduces another argument and counter-argument, supported by an **added** point. Copy out the section below and annotate it to show where each of these features occurs and comment on their effectiveness.

> It would be stupid to think that we are all so weak-willed that we 'share our unhealthy food with our new friends' to be 'one of the crowd'. What could be more generous than sharing something that YOU REALLY WANT with your new friends?

2 When you are writing to persuade, it is important to **think about the effect on the reader** or listener. This will help you to decide whether the persuasive techniques that you are using will have the right impact on the audience. Pick out examples of the following persuasive techniques in the model speech:

- rhetorical questions that involve listeners and make them think
- lists of three that powerfully emphasise the point being made
- repetition to highlight particular ideas
- use of 'we' to encourage the audience to share the speaker's viewpoint.

Remember to use these techniques when you are writing your own persuasive speech.

3 Vocabulary techniques such as exaggeration, alliteration and imagery are often used in persuasive writing to contribute to the persuasive **effect on the reader**. Copy and complete the table below, explaining what effect each example from the speech might have on the listener.

Technique	Example	Effect on the reader
Alliteration	Sick of **s**ad **s**alad	Draws attention to the phrase and creates a negative sound effect which undermines the healthy eating promoted by the Healthy Hut.
Imagery (metaphor) and exaggeration	Taste nectar at the gates of heaven	
Action and imperative verbs	**Spice up** your life – **come** to the Chocolate Chamber. **Indulge**! **Spoil** yourself!	
Colloquialisms and informal language	Well, now you can **have your cake and eat it** – without guilt! Guilt's a most over-rated **trip** anyway	

Planning to write

Interesting texts

1 a You are going to write another paragraph to add to the model speech. Look back at the fishbone plan that you created on page 114. Choose one argument from the Healthy Hut flyer and your linked counter-argument that you would like to add to the speech.

b Think of a point to **add** to your counter-argument that will help you to strengthen your main point and make it more persuasive. Make notes on this to help you when writing your paragraph.

2 a Remember that you are going to be **writing for a listener** in order to persuade them to buy chocolate cakes from you. You could be writing for listeners who used to eat chocolate but have been trying to eat healthily, or listeners who really do like the healthy food offered in the Healthy Hut. It often helps to write for someone if you can picture them in your mind. What do you imagine your listeners doing and thinking?

b Can you **add** anything to your plan to help you to keep your listeners in mind as you write? Does the picture of your listener affect how you will make your argument?

Composing

Interesting texts

1 a Now write your paragraph to add to the speech to your school assembly.

- Start by stating the original argument from the Healthy Hut flyer, making it clear to what extent you agree or disagree with it.

- Next, you will need to explain your counter-argument that focuses on why the Chocolate Chamber is necessary. You will need to contrast this point with the argument from the Healthy Hut flyer.

- Now develop your counter-argument by **adding** a further point for real persuasive impact. You could make it sound important by introducing it with a phrase such as 'most importantly' or 'what is more'.

b As you add each piece of information, **loop back** and re-read what you have just written, asking yourself 'What is the **effect on the listener**?' Try to use some of the persuasive techniques that you explored in the model speech. For example, could you use a rhetorical question to add to the persuasive impact?

Improving

Range of punctuation

1 a The text of the speech is going to be printed in the weekly school newsletter, so it will be important that punctuation is used accurately to make the meaning clear and that a variety of different punctuation marks is used effectively. Re-read the model speech, focusing on the range of punctuation used. Copy and complete the table below, finding an example of the use of each of the punctuation marks listed and explaining why these are used in each case.

Range of punctuation	Example	Why this is used
Exclamation mark		
Question mark		
Ellipsis		
Dash		

b Now look at the punctuation in your paragraph. Check that you have used punctuation marks accurately. Are there any places where you could use some of the punctuation marks used in the model text? What impact would this have on your writing?

▶ Reviewing

1 a Swap your paragraph with a partner. Answer the following questions about their writing:

- Which persuasive techniques have they used? What is the **effect** of each of these **on the listener**?

- What punctuation marks have they used? Why have they chosen to use these in their paragraph?

b Write down one piece of advice for your partner to try next time they write a persuasive text. Explain how this will help them to improve the effectiveness of their writing.

Task 2 Cold comfort?

Without consulting parents or pupils, the catering company that provides your school dinners has recently changed its menu so that only cold salads are served. You have been asked by your year group to represent them at a meeting with the catering company that has been arranged to discuss the recent changes.

The main concerns of your year group are that:

- Many of you often go to school without any breakfast and salads just won't keep you going during the day.

- For some pupils, the only chance of a hot meal is at school.

- You need a balanced diet and this menu won't offer enough carbohydrates.

Write a speech to deliver at the meeting to the head of catering to persuade the company to reintroduce the previous menu.

Planning to write

Interesting texts

1 a Remember that when writing a speech to persuade you need to **write for a listener**. This task is different from the first task in this unit because you are writing for a different audience. In pairs, discuss what differences between the two audiences (your whole school assembly and the head of catering) you will need to consider when writing this speech.

b Re-read the model speech on page 115 and identify which techniques used create the informal tone. Which of these techniques would still be suitable for this speech to the head of catering? Which of them should you try to avoid using?

c Copy and complete the table below to help you remember the key points you need to think about when completing this task. Look back at the version of this table you completed for Task 1 on page 114 if you need to remind yourself about what details to include.

	Information in the task	What this means I need to do
Viewpoint		
Purpose		
Audience		
Content		

2   In this task, the concerns of your year group should be the main focus of your counter-arguments. You will need to decide what arguments the catering company would make for the changes they have made, so that your counter-arguments will be effective. In pairs, create a fishbone plan for this task. Look carefully at the information in the task and list each of the counter-arguments that you are going to use to persuade the catering company to change the menu.

- Discuss what arguments the catering company would make to support their new menu. For each of your counter-arguments note down the argument that this is challenging.

- Then return to your counter-arguments and expand these points so that there is enough detail for you to **add** further points to make your speech more persuasive.

- Decide on the order in which you will present your points.

Composing

Interesting texts

1   You are now going to work individually to write a speech to persuade the head of catering to change the school menu.

   a   Start by writing an introduction that clearly states your opinion and the reason for making this speech. The tone you create should be polite, but make your demands clear. Remember that you are writing to persuade rather than simply to complain because you want to convince them to make changes.

   b   Introduce your first point. Think about how you are going to use your counter-argument. You might state the catering company's argument in order to criticise it or you might agree with it in part but want to suggest a change to part of it.

   c   For extra persuasive impact, remember to **add** a further point to your counter-argument.

d As you write, make sure your viewpoint remains clear and consistent throughout. To do this, you need to **loop back** as you compose your speech, to re-read what you have written and **think about the effect on the listener**. Check that your argument is advancing in a logical way and that the tone is appropriate for the listener. Remember that your writing needs to be formal: you want the head of catering to take you seriously.

e Repeat this sequence for each of the remaining points on your fishbone plan. In your final paragraph you should restate your main argument and expectations about what will happen next.

Improving

Range of punctuation

1 a You have been asked to leave a printed copy of your speech with the head of catering after the meeting so you need to check your punctuation. Read through your speech and check that you have:

- accurately used the right punctuation marks
- used punctuation to communicate your meaning clearly to the reader
- included a range of different punctuation marks.

b Work with a partner to make the necessary changes to improve the clarity of your writing and the range of techniques used.

▶ Reviewing

1 a Review your speech by completing a copy of this table.

Have I:	Yes	No	A little
Adapted my style to suit the purpose and audience of the task, for example used the right level of formality?			
Used counter-arguments effectively?			
Added ideas to strengthen my points?			
Used appropriate persuasive techniques, for example rhetorical questions, lists of three, imagery, imperative verbs?			

b Look at the columns where you have placed your ticks. Revisit your work where you have ticked the 'A little' column. What changes could you make to your work to move these ticks to the 'Yes' column?

c Now focus on the ticks in the 'No' column. These are areas for you to improve next time. Make sure that you understand how to use each of these techniques.

New worlds

Inform, explain, describe

When you are writing to inform, explain and describe, you need to guide the reader clearly through the text. This means that the organisation of the information is very important. Newspaper reports are an example of this type of writing. They give information, but they might also explain events and opinions and describe what has happened. The paragraphs in newspaper reports each have specific functions. In this unit you will practise planning the structure of newspaper reports and use different ways of making links between ideas and paragraphs.

Writing strategies

- see the whole text
- choose how to plan
- loop back

Pre-writing: see the whole text

1   You are a reporter on your school newspaper. You have been asked to give advice to new reporters about how to structure the content of a newspaper report. These are the questions they have asked:

- What information should I give in the headline?

- What goes in the first paragraph and how does this help the organisation of the information in the report?

- How should I organise the details about the main events?

- Where do I include comments from people involved?

- How could I end the report?

Think about newspaper reports you have seen or written yourself. Discuss the questions with a partner and decide what advice you would give to the new reporters.

Jungle fever

Your next assignment for your school newspaper is to write a report on the activities and achievements of students who have recently left school. You have received the following information:

- A group of students has just returned from a jungle expedition.
- The students raised £3,000 for charity.
- Their adventures included snake bites, jungle fever and a near-drowning experience.

Write a report for your school newspaper, informing readers about the jungle expedition.

Before you begin to write your report for the school newspaper about this expedition, the editor reminds you of the following key points:

- Purpose – to inform readers about the jungle expedition.
- Audience – teachers, parents and pupils. The writing should be lively and enthusiastic and include information of interest to the different readers of the newspaper.
- Content – you have been given the main points but you need to find out more details to include.
- Viewpoint – you are representing your school so you need to take a positive view of the events.

Studying a report

Interesting texts

1 The students who have returned from the jungle expedition are going to take part in a press conference where they will explain what they did and how they felt about the different things that happened. Working in a group, create the character of one of the students. Prepare some questions to ask at the press conference and rehearse the answers the student might give.

Organising the ideas

2 After the press conference, one of the new reporters e-mails their report to you. Unfortunately a computer virus has changed the order of the paragraphs in the report below. Discuss in your group the appropriate order for each of the paragraphs. Remember, you will need to give reasons for the decisions you make.

3 Think back to the advice you prepared for new reporters about how to organise information in a newspaper report. Does this report follow your rules?

Students come out of Africa

The three ex-students are looking forward to a quiet week or two at home but at the beginning of next term they will be in school to give a slideshow in assembly. Mr Tenner, the headteacher, said: 'We are incredibly proud of them and know that their experiences will be an inspiration to other young people in this school.'

Three students completed a ten-day trek through the African jungle to raise money for charity. Ben Nichol, 17, Orla Jones, 18, and Nicky Lemmon, also 18, flew in to Heathrow yesterday having undertaken a ten-day expedition, facing deadly snake bites, risky river crossings and potentially fatal jungle fever.

The expedition not only raised money for charity but also provided Ben, Orla and Nicky with a life-changing experience. Tanned and excited, although exhausted from the long flight back, they could not stop talking: 'It was unbelievable – terrifying but also exhilarating,' laughed Orla. 'Ben was bitten by a snake and I went down with a fever …' There were a few more hair-raising moments too, including a perilous river crossing and an encounter with an army of ants.

Check the school website for more info and pics.

Lizzie Jones, 52, mother of Orla, said it had been a nerve-racking time for the family. 'It was an amazing experience for her, but I worried all the time she was away. It was so good to see her back safe and sound.' The parents of the students and some of their friends went to the airport to welcome the travellers home. Wayne Files, Gita Patel and Billy Neep, who had been in the same year group as the adventurers, made a banner to greet them with and carried balloons with their names on. Wayne, who, like all the ex-students, is currently waiting for his A-level results, said, 'It was a great thing they did. I really admire them. I would have gone but I can't stand creepy-crawlies!'

The three friends planned the expedition for 18 months beforehand. Ben was the driving force behind it: his little brother is disabled and uses a wheelchair. To do sports, however, which Jack, aged 8, loves, he needs a specially adapted wheelchair. These cost six thousand pounds each and there was no way that Ben and Jack's parents could afford to buy one. Tom Nichol, who works for the local council, said, 'It broke my heart but I had to say no. We just don't have that kind of money.' The charity Kidzwheelz offered to pay half the cost if the family could raise the other half.

Paragraphs and links

4 Look at the beginning of each paragraph. Identify how each paragraph opening links back to a reference earlier in the text by copying out and completing the following table.

Quotation	Links back to ...	How the link works
'Lizzie Jones, 52, mother of Orla ...'	'Orla Jones' in the first paragraph.	As we read the phrase, we immediately make the link to the surname. The age confirms that it is likely to be an older relative of Orla's, then the status of mother is revealed.
'The three friends ...'		

5 What other links within the text can you find?

   a Pick out examples of the synonyms (words or phrases with the same meaning) the reporter uses for 'the three students' and their 'expedition'. Why do you think the writer uses synonyms in this report?

   b What use does the writer make of the technique of substituting pronouns for nouns? What effect does this have?

   c Which connectives does the writer use to make links between the information?

6 **See the whole text**. Create a snapshot of the shape and organisation of the whole text. Describe to a partner what you can see. Good writers hold this picture in their head as they write.

Planning to write

Organising the ideas

1 **Choose how to plan**. In a group, discuss how the report you have studied might have been planned. What might the plan have looked like? How much detail might have been included?

2 Start by reviewing the key ideas for your newspaper report. Then, with a partner, try to **see the whole text** and discuss how the main details will be organised before creating your plan. Annotate and adapt your plan to show how you will organise these ideas and comments. For example, you could number the points or create a diagram to show the order of the information and how it will be grouped into paragraphs.

Composing

Paragraphs and links

1 The opening paragraph should say who, what, when, where and why. Check how the report on page 124 does this. Using your plan, draft the opening paragraph of your report. In pairs, compare your openings with the report on page 124.

2 Identify the content of the second paragraph from your plan. Think of three different ways you could start this paragraph. In pairs, discuss which you think is best and why.

3 Write the second sentence of the paragraph and highlight the link to the previous sentence. Compare sentences across the class and make a list of the different ways of making links. Now add the other points to make in this paragraph and think about how the paragraph should end.

4 In pairs, continue writing the report. As you add each piece of information, use the **looping back** writing strategy. Re-read what you have just written and talk to each other about how you are making links across the text. Refer to your plan and the notes you have made on different ways of linking ideas together.

▶ Reviewing

1 Swap work with another pair.

   a Highlight where each paragraph links back to earlier in the text and the links between sentences.

   b Underline any places where you think better links could have been made and explain your advice to your partner.

2 Great news! Your work on the school newspaper has been recognised. Now, a national newspaper wants you to write a report for its front page! Before you attend the briefing at the newspaper's London office, you decide to check how to write a really good report. Make a checklist of the key points you need to remember.

3 Think about the last report you wrote. What did you need to improve? How will you get it right this time? What help do you need to achieve this?

LW Task 2 Landing on the red planet

The national newspaper has asked you to write a report on the landing of the first manned space flight to Mars.

Mars landing

- Wednesday 3.23 am spaceship landed on Mars
- Astronauts went walkabout on the surface of Mars
- One astronaut said: 'It's incredible – it doesn't look red – but a sort of muddy brown.'

Write a newspaper report informing readers about the Mars landing.

Planning to write

Organising the ideas

1 **Choose how to plan**. Look at the planning page below that the national newspaper has provided to help you get started. What else do you need to think about as you prepare your ideas for this report? Adapt the plan to include the organisation of the ideas in the main part of the report.

2 **See the whole text**. What is your report going to look like? Picture in your head the key features of the organisation. Remember to refer back to this picture as you write.

Planning page

Headline:

Opening paragraph

Ideas for report

Comments from other people

Ending

Composing

Paragraphs and links

1 **Loop back.** As your draft your report, keep re-reading what you have written to check the progression of your ideas and give yourself time to think about how to link them together.

2 Use a variety of ways of linking your ideas:

- substitution (for example, replace nouns with pronouns)
- connectives
- synonyms.

▶ Reviewing

1 The editor is happy with your report, but wants to meet you to review your work and consider your future. You are keen to impress, so you decide to prepare for this meeting by annotating your report.

a Have you followed the advice you prepared for the new reporters and your own checklist?

b Highlight the links made between paragraphs and sentences in your own work.

c Identify any places where you could have made a better link.

d Compare your report with the first one you wrote. What do you think you have done better this time?

2 Identify one aspect of organising a newspaper report that you want to improve next time. The following list might help you to make your choice:

- Structure the whole report in an interesting way.
- Group information logically into paragraphs.
- Organise ideas within paragraphs.
- In the introduction, identify the main points of the report but leave details to be developed later.
- Conclude the report with comments that reflect on the wider issues raised by the events reported.
- Use a range of synonyms to provide variety while still making links for the reader.
- Use pronouns to replace nouns to ensure you aren't repeating yourself, but avoid ambiguity.

Moving about

Analyse, review, comment

When writing to analyse, review or comment, you need to be able to balance a range of views, including your own. An analysis is a piece of writing that explores an issue, but hands the responsibility to the reader to form his or her own view of the problem. Writing an analysis is often a difficult skill since you need to present viewpoints, with which you don't necessarily agree, in a fair way. In this unit you will explore how using connectives and other cohesive devices within paragraphs can help to produce a detailed and balanced analysis. You will also practise writing concisely to time limits to improve the skills you need when writing in tests and exams.

Writing strategies

- choose how to plan
- use your plan
- changing

Pre-writing: choose how to plan

1   In this unit, you will analyse the problem of how pupils travel to and from school and write a report about this. When you are producing a piece of writing in a test or exam, you need to be able to choose the most appropriate planning technique and use this to help you to plan quickly. Use the table below to help you to create a simple plan, making brief notes on the main points for and against the different types of transport that pupils use to get to school. The first row has been started for you.

Form of transport	Good points	Bad points
Bicycle	• environmentally friendly •	• nowhere to store bike safely •

Getting to school

Traffic around schools is a big problem, especially at the beginning of the day.

Your headteacher has asked pupils to write a report analysing the benefits and drawbacks of the different forms of transport pupils could use to travel to school instead of by car.

Think about:
- the different forms of transport pupils have to choose from
- the reasons that pupils are more likely to come by car than use an alternative method of transport
- what the headteacher needs to consider when choosing which forms of transport to encourage.

Write a report for the headteacher analysing the different forms of transport pupils could use to travel to school.

Look again at the writing task and think about:

- Purpose – to explore alternatives to travelling to school by car. The report should help your reader to understand pupils' needs and think about which forms of transport to encourage.

- Audience – your headteacher and other adults in the school community, for example governors.

- Structure – the report should begin with an overview of the issues to be considered and what criteria will be used to analyse the alternatives, for example safety or cost. The body of the report should discuss each alternative in turn, referring to the criteria, and following the structure of point, evidence then comment or development. It should end with a brief conclusion, summarising the issues analysed.

- Style – the style should be formal and impartial, presenting evidence fairly and balancing different viewpoints.

Studying a report

Here is a report that another pupil has completed analysing the issue.

In considering the reasons why some pupils choose to travel to school by car rather than other methods of transport, there are many things to reflect on. Since there are many reasons why pupils come by car instead of walking, cycling or coming by bus, the report below should allow you to think about how you might begin to encourage pupils to choose other methods of transport instead.

Cycling to school is one method pupils could consider for getting to school. Whilst this is a relatively cheap and environmentally friendly form of transport, at the moment there is nowhere for pupils to store the bicycles. This means that they could easily be stolen when pupils are in lessons, since they have to leave them chained to the school railings. Most bike locks are easy to pick, and some bikes have been stolen as a result.

Another reason cycling is not more popular is that there is nowhere in school for pupils to shower. If they come some distance by bike, there is nowhere for them to wash, and they have to spend all day feeling sweaty and dirty. You would have to take these factors into consideration if you were thinking of promoting cycling.

A slightly less environmentally friendly method of transport would be to come by bus. Here, some pupils choose to come to school by car because there are no local buses that can take them to school, and it is therefore very inconvenient. Although buses can carry many pupils together, which would reduce the traffic, some of our younger pupils are too afraid to get on the bus, as they are afraid of being bullied. As one Year 7 says: "Some of the Year 10 pupils bully me and call me names when I get on the bus. That's why my mum brings me by car." Some of our pupils feel very unsafe on the buses; consequently, you would have to consider ways to make sure our younger students feel secure on school bus runs.

Walking is a more popular method of arriving at school for some pupils who live in close proximity to the school grounds. Whilst this is the most healthy and environmentally friendly way of getting to school, many pupils have several lessons where they need to bring books and heavy equipment. Have you thought of how you might make it easier for pupils to keep some things in school so that they didn't have as much to carry? When we have PE and Art or Design and Technology on the same day, we may need to bring more than one bag. This may make pupils choose to come by car, if they can, so they don't have to lug all their equipment with them. Another reason pupils say they choose to come to school by car when they could walk is that on days when it is very wet and windy, or very cold, they would spend all day drying out and warming up. As I'm sure you'll appreciate, England is a very wet, windy, cold place for at least half the year, so it may be very difficult to encourage a child to walk when they see it is raining and their mum is happy to give them a lift.

In conclusion, I think you will need to think carefully about the incentives you offer to pupils who walk, cycle or come by bus, before you decide to make it more difficult for pupils to come by car. If you decide to encourage any other method of transport, you will need to decide how you will share this with pupils, as, at present, they have more reasons to come by car than any other method of transport. You might want to consider incentives or rewards to promote other forms of transport other than cars.

Paragraphs and links

1   Re-read each paragraph of the report. Working with a partner, summarise what each paragraph is about in ten or fewer words. Then pick out the words in the paragraph that helped you to decide this.

2   Look again at the three middle paragraphs of the report. The writer has used different devices, including connectives, repeated phrases and repeated sentence structures, to link the ideas in these paragraphs.

    a   Look at the way the writer has used repetition of vocabulary and sentence structures. What words and phrases are repeated? Discuss with your partner why you think the writer has used this technique.

    b   Look at how each paragraph is organised. The annotations below show how the writer has organised the points about one type of transport, balancing different viewpoints and using connectives to link the sentences together. How have the same techniques been used in the paragraphs about travelling by bus and walking?

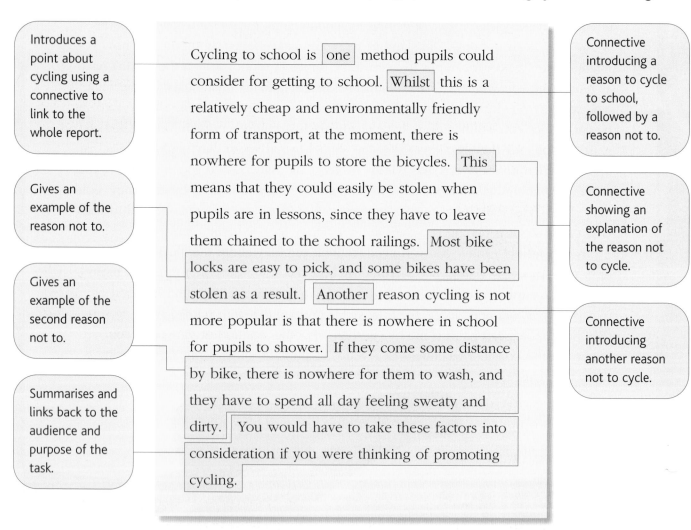

Introduces a point about cycling using a connective to link to the whole report.

Gives an example of the reason not to.

Gives an example of the second reason not to.

Summarises and links back to the audience and purpose of the task.

Cycling to school is one method pupils could consider for getting to school. Whilst this is a relatively cheap and environmentally friendly form of transport, at the moment, there is nowhere for pupils to store the bicycles. This means that they could easily be stolen when pupils are in lessons, since they have to leave them chained to the school railings. Most bike locks are easy to pick, and some bikes have been stolen as a result. Another reason cycling is not more popular is that there is nowhere in school for pupils to shower. If they come some distance by bike, there is nowhere for them to wash, and they have to spend all day feeling sweaty and dirty. You would have to take these factors into consideration if you were thinking of promoting cycling.

Connective introducing a reason to cycle to school, followed by a reason not to.

Connective showing an explanation of the reason not to cycle.

Connective introducing another reason not to cycle.

3   Now look at the final paragraph and pick out the different connectives the writer uses. What is the purpose of this final paragraph?

4   Think about the purpose and audience of this report. What has the writer done to make sure that the style and tone are appropriate? How has the writer shown that they have considered a range of viewpoints?

Planning to write

Paragraphs and links

1   Think about how the writer might have planned their work by 'reverse' planning.

a   **Choose how to plan** by selecting an appropriate planning format. Add to the plan details about the purpose of the writing, the viewpoints represented and the style of language. Now add the main topics of each paragraph.

b   Add to the plan the connectives and paragraph links the writer uses to join the different sections of the report together.

c   You should now be able to see the 'skeleton' plan behind the writer's report. Think about using this type of plan when you write your own analytical report.

2   a   Look back at the table you created in the pre-writing task on page 129 and choose another form of transport that you made notes on. Then write a list of three or four different points about the use of this type of transport, some for and some against.

b   Now sort these notes into a linked order. Experiment by numbering the points on your list in different ways to decide on the most effective order.

c   When you have decided on an order, write out the points in the order you want to use them. Then add to your plan connective words and phrases to lead from one sentence to the next. You should now have a detailed plan that will help you when you start to draft your report. Use this technique to plan the other paragraphs in your report.

Composing

Paragraphs and links

1   **Use your plan.** Look back at your plan and think about it before you begin to write each paragraph. As you write each sentence, tick off the point you have made and the connective used from your plan. This should help you make sure that you don't repeat any points unnecessarily and that you use a range of connectives.

▶ Reviewing

1   You are now going to take the team spelling challenge. The team with the lowest score wins!

a   Working in a team of five or six, swap your reports with another team. As a team, scan through the reports, highlighting any spelling errors. Each error correctly identified adds one point to the other team's total. However, if you wrongly identify any spelling errors, you will have two points added to your team's total, so use a dictionary or spellchecker to help you.

b   You will repeat this challenge after your next task, so consider any spelling errors you made and think of ways of remembering the correct spellings.

Two wheels or feet

The governors of your school want to encourage pupils who live near to the school to walk or cycle rather than coming by car. They have come up with several proposals to encourage walking and cycling, and they would like you to explore the advantages and disadvantages of their ideas.

The proposals to encourage walking and cycling are to:

- start a breakfast club for pupils who walk or cycle
- build secure bike sheds
- encourage 'walking' teams of pupils who walk to school together
- reward pupils who regularly walk or cycle to school with a trip out to a theme park.

Write your report for the school governors analysing these proposals.

Planning to write

Organising the ideas

1 a With a partner, discuss the purpose and audience of this task. What will you need to include to make sure that your report is appropriate?

b Choose how to plan. It is helpful to be able to plan quickly and concisely when you have only a set time for your writing. Spend exactly five minutes to create a paragraph plan including this information:

- different viewpoints about each proposal
- introductory ideas and introductory connectives
- three or four main ideas to form each paragraph
- connectives to show links within each of these paragraphs
- connectives to link each paragraph to the next
- concluding ideas and summarising connectives.

c Work as quickly as you can. Once the five minutes are up, stop and change to a different coloured pen, before finishing your plan off and adding any other details. When you have finished planning, look at where you spent time on your plan. Did you start quickly and not add very much after the time limit ended? Were you slow to start but then added lots of detail later? What are your strengths and weaknesses in planning when you have a limited amount of time?

Composing

Paragraphs and links

1 The school governors are meeting today so have given you 25 minutes to write your report. When writing, **use your plan** to help you keep a tight focus on your report.

   a Remember to include your connectives to help the reader move from one paragraph to the next in a fluid way. Look back at the work you did on Task 1 to remind yourself of other devices you can use to create links within your writing, for example repeated vocabulary and sentence structures. Try to use these in your report.

   b Make sure you have connectives linking the sentences in each paragraph so that your ideas are not disjointed.

2 When the 25 minutes are up, you may continue writing if you need to, but use a different coloured pen. This will help you know how much you write in a set time and think about whether you need to speed up or not.

Improving

Correct spelling

1 Before you take the team spelling challenge again, re-read your report and check any spellings of which you are unsure. **Change** any words you think might need correcting and underline any about which you are still unsure. Predict the individual score your report would receive in the team spelling challenge.

▶ Reviewing

1 Working in the same teams as before, swap your reports and carry out the team spelling challenge. Your teacher may set you a team target to beat. Remember, the lower the score, the better. How did your team's score compare with the score you got last time?

2 Look again at your report and compare your predicted individual score with the one you received. Were you better, the same, or worse than you thought you would be?

3 Think about the areas you have worked on in this unit:

- choosing ways to plan
- using your plan to guide your writing
- planning and writing under timed conditions
- checking your spelling.

What are your strengths and weaknesses in each area? At the bottom of your report, note two targets for your next piece of writing.

15 Heroes

Persuade, argue, advise

When writing to persuade, argue or advise, you should always consider your audience and think about how formal or informal your writing needs to be. A successful argument is well organised as well as being varied in the way it appeals to the reader. In this unit you will explore the different techniques used when writing to argue. You will also consider how word choice affects formality.

Writing strategies

- write for a reader
- think about the effect on the reader
- choose how to plan
- adding
- changing

Pre-writing: write for a reader

1 a Letters to the editor of a newspaper, letters of complaint and magazine articles that present a case are all examples of writing to argue. Can you think of any times when you have written to argue?

b When you write to argue, you are expressing your views on the issue concerned. You might do this to let someone know your views when you feel strongly about something or perhaps to actually influence somebody to change an outcome in your favour. To do this effectively, you also need to think about who you are writing for and how that affects the way you need to write.

For each feature of writing to argue listed in the table on the opposite page, tick the relevant box to show which you feel confident you could use (green), which you are fairly confident about using (amber) and which you are not confident about using (red).

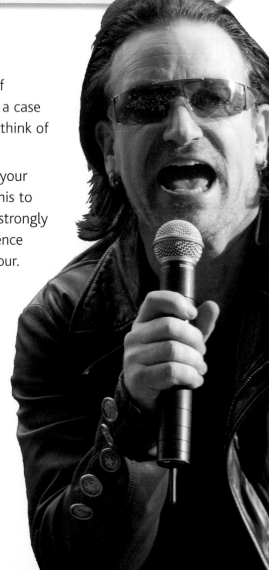

Features of writing to argue	Green	Amber	Red
Reaffirm your purpose throughout			
State opinions as if they were facts			
Use complex sentences to present, echo and oppose ideas			
Link paragraphs effectively			
Use argumentative techniques, such as:			

Use argumentative techniques, such as:

- lists of three
- rhetorical questions
- repetition
- abstract nouns
- exaggerated adjectives

Choose appropriate formal vocabulary

Close with a summary of your arguments

LW Task 1

We can be heroes

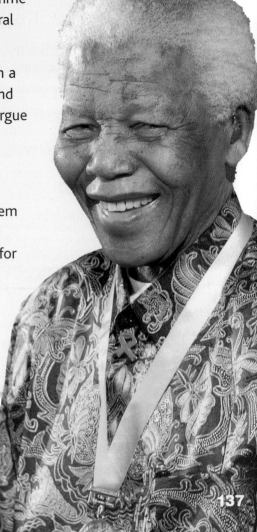

A national television channel is planning a programme called 'Inspiring Individuals' and is asking the general public to nominate their favourite famous hero.

To enter the event, you have been asked to send in a letter saying who your favourite famous hero is, and why you have nominated them. You will need to argue that your hero deserves to be included in the programme.

Think about:
- who your hero is and how you can describe them
- what they have done that has influenced you
- why you think they are an inspiring individual for others as well as yourself.

Write a letter to the programme makers arguing that your hero should be included in the 'Inspiring Individuals' programme.

Studying a letter that argues a point of view

1 Here is a letter that the 'Inspiring Individuals' programme makers have already received. Before you read the letter, discuss with a partner the purpose and audience. How formal do you think this letter should be? What features of writing would you expect to see? How should the ideas and arguments be organised?

Dear Sir,

In regard to your upcoming television programme, 'Inspiring Individuals', I would like to nominate Martin Johnson, the captain of the World Cup-winning rugby union team. Whilst others may nominate individuals who are more of a personal choice, I think Martin Johnson should be featured on your show because I am sure his inspiration goes far. Although some nominees will, I am sure, be more famous than the individual I have chosen, it is possibly his understated personal qualities that make him stand out from the rest. These qualities sometimes mean that others receive more merit than he does for their achievements, and I would like to see him take his place among the most inspirational people of our time, as I am sure he deserves it.

When watching Martin Johnson playing rugby, it is very easy not to notice him at all, despite the fact he is six foot seven and weighs eighteen stone! But it is in his quiet presence and gritty determination that I find the most inspiration from him. He may not be the world's most talented or dynamic player, yet his personal strengths carried him and the England team to victory in Sydney in 2003. It is these strengths that I find the most admirable. It is what I respect in him. He shows that you do not need to be the person who gets all the fame and glory from scoring or creating great sporting moments, but that glory comes from knowing you were part of a successful team. He is generous in praising others, yet modest about his own impact. Although many people will remember Jonny Wilkinson's famous drop goal in the last moments of the World Cup final, few will remember the vital yards Johnson gained before sending the ball to Matt Dawson, then on to Wilkinson, who will live on in sporting history as the man who won the World Cup for England. It is precisely this modesty that deserves to be rewarded in acknowledging his achievements by taking part in your 'Inspiring Individuals' programme. To me, it is his solid performance and steely determination that make him a hero.

Whilst it is easy to get discouraged when things don't seem to be going your way, I think the fact that Martin Johnson never shows he feels defeated is the one thing I admire the most about him. The way he never gives up and never gives in is surely inspirational to us all. If only we all had such persistence and determination! The way he battles on when things seem as bad as they possibly could be is something we should not just appreciate, but something we should celebrate. After all, without his vital ground-gaining battling in every single moment of the World Cup tournament, where would the England rugby union team be?

It is also this constant quest for his personal best that inspires those around him. It inspires me too. It is no wonder, to me, that all his teammates recognise his contributions on the pitch. His personal determination and persistence captured the whole team. Perhaps it is the attitude he puts across that is also something to admire, because everybody around him seems to share his team-focussed approach and never-quitting persistence when he is on the pitch.

The way he leads by example and acts as a role model for those around him is also inspirational. In a world where footballers are splattered across the front pages of the tabloids with various sordid tales of adultery, loutish behaviour and arrogance both on and off the pitch, I think it is something to celebrate that we have individuals who are sportsman-like off the pitch as well as on it. When bad behaviour is rewarded with lots of publicity, shouldn't outstanding actions be rewarded once in a while too?

I would like you to feature our most successful rugby union captain in 'Inspiring Individuals' because of the work he does off the pitch as well as on it. Is it not something to celebrate when someone does something remarkable and totally unselfish for those around them? He is a wonderful role model for any child.

Taking all this into account, I hope you can see why Martin Johnson is an inspiration to all those around him. It is his determination, his presence, his persistence and his quest for his own personal best that make him my hero. If only everyone shared some of these qualities, the world would surely be a better place. Please celebrate his achievements by accepting this nomination for 'Inspiring Individuals'.

Yours faithfully,

Jenny Smith

Using different text types

2 a When writing to argue, writers often make assertions by stating opinions as if they are facts. Scan the letter for examples of assertions. What effect does it have on the argument to suggest an opinion as though it is a fact?

b Sometimes, writers suggest opinions to the reader rather than stating them as definite facts. One way of doing this is to use modal verbs that suggest possibilities (e.g. might, may, could). Identify examples of the use of this technique in the letter.

3 a Each paragraph includes a sentence that reaffirms the purpose of the letter for the reader. For example, 'It is also this constant quest for his personal best that inspires those around him' at the start of the fourth paragraph. Which sentences in the second and third paragraphs make links back to the purpose of the letter?

b How does the writer avoid direct repetition in these sentences, yet make it clear each time what the purpose of the letter is?

4 Look at this complex sentence from the third paragraph, which ends with two phrases that echo one another:

> The way he battles on when things seem as bad as they possibly could be is something we should not just appreciate, but something we should celebrate.

a Re-read the letter and pick out examples of the use of echoed words and ideas. Why is this an effective technique to use when writing to argue?

b Copy out and complete the following table to help you explore how the writer has created balance in the letter by opposing ideas in sentences.

Example	Effect on the reader
'Whilst others ... , I think ...'	
'He may not be ..., yet ...'	
'Although many people will remember ..., few will remember ...'	

5 a The last sentence of each paragraph is linked to the first sentence of the next paragraph. Identify how these links are created between the third, fourth and fifth paragraphs.

  a How do these links help to prepare the reader for the content of the next paragraph? How do these sentences help to make the whole letter seem cohesive?

6 The final paragraph summarises the reasons why the writer believes Martin Johnson should be included in the 'Inspiring Individuals' programme. How does the writer use the final paragraph to reinforce the points made earlier in the letter?

7 Read the whole letter again and identify any other argumentative features that the writer has used, such as lists of three, repetition and rhetorical questions. Pick out as many examples as you can find of each. For each example, explain how this technique helps the writer to express her ideas in a powerful way.

Choice of vocabulary

8 The writer has used many abstract nouns in her letter: 'inspiration', 'fame', 'glory', 'presence' and 'determination'. Abstract nouns refer to ideas, concepts and other unmeasurable things, so when writing about a person you need to use abstract nouns to help you to present aspects of their personality and qualities which aren't concrete as part of your argument.

    a Pick out another abstract noun the writer has used in paragraph two.

    b Adding an adjective to an abstract noun can make these more powerful. For example, 'never-quitting persistence' is more powerful than 'persistence' on its own. Add an adjective to the abstract noun you have picked out to make it more powerful.

9 The writer has chosen to use a formal style for this letter.

    a In the introduction, the writer uses the phrase 'In regard to' to introduce the context for the letter. What formal vocabulary has the writer selected in the final paragraph to introduce the context?

    b Pick out other examples of formal vocabulary used throughout the letter. Is the level of formality always constant? For example, think about the effect of using exclamation marks.

Planning to write

Using different text types

1 a You are now going to create a plan for your own letter to the 'Inspiring Individuals' programme makers. Decide which famous hero you would like to nominate.

    b Although you don't know your reader personally, you can still successfully **write for a reader** by working out what the reader needs to know. Make a list of what you think the programme makers will expect the letter to contain.

    c **Choose how to plan**. You need to choose a format that will help you organise your ideas into paragraphs and develop points within each paragraph. Include examples you can use to support each of your chosen celebrity's qualities in your plan. Remember to use abstract nouns.

Choice of vocabulary

2 Planning how to use words effectively will also help you to **write for a reader**. Remember that your choice of vocabulary needs to be formal.

    a Add to your plan abstract nouns that you can use to describe the qualities of your chosen inspiring individual and think of adjectives you can use to expand these in more detail.

    b Add ideas to your plan about how you are going to argue your case. Think about the different features of writing to argue that you could use, for example rhetorical questions and lists of three.

Composing

Using different text types

1 Choose one paragraph from your plan to draft first, making sure you **think about the effect on the reader**. As you write, think about the different techniques you will use to argue your case and structure your letter: assertions, argumentative techniques, linked paragraphs, complex sentences and reaffirmations of purpose. In particular, focus on the techniques you felt less confident about at the beginning of this unit.

Choice of vocabulary

2 As you write your paragraph, think about the following:

- including abstract nouns to describe your hero's qualities
- **adding** adjectives to make the nouns more powerful.

3 The vocabulary you choose and the construction of your sentences need to be formal. To help you maintain the right level of formality, **think about the effect on the reader**. As you write, make sure you maintain an appropriate formal tone for your audience. Are you creating a tone that will make them take your arguments seriously?

4 Now draft the rest of your letter.

▶ Reviewing

1   When you have finished your first draft, look back at what you have written. Go through and highlight all your abstract nouns. Have you included adjectives around them to build them up into noun phrases to describe your hero's qualities in a powerful way? **Add** more adjectives to your writing.

2   Check your writing thoroughly to make sure you have used the right tense throughout. Have you stayed with the same tense? Where you have changed tense, is this deliberate?

3   Which features of writing to argue have you used successfully? Look back at the list of features in the table on page 137. Annotate your work to show where you have used each of these features.

4   Review the annotations you have made on your letter. Discuss with a partner whether there are any techniques you didn't use, or that you think you could use more effectively. Target these in the next task to make sure you are using the full range of techniques to argue your case.

We all need a hero

A competition has been launched in your local newspaper to find the unsung heroes of the United Kingdom. The newspaper editor has asked readers to write in nominating their local unsung hero and these letters will be published in the newspaper. Readers will then vote on who should win the overall award. The editor has included the statement about the competition opposite:

It's that time of year when we are looking to celebrate the achievements of the great and the good. Don't forget: heroes don't have to be household names. They can be teachers, nurses, charity workers and relatives – or just somebody who has shown courage in difficult circumstances. That's why we are asking for your nominations.

Write a letter to the editor nominating your unsung hero. You should argue why your hero is deserving of the award and how they are more influential than other individuals. Remember – your hero should be someone you know individually, rather than a celebrity.

Planning to write

Using different text types

1 **Write for a reader.** Before you start, think about the following questions:
   - Who is the audience for your letter?
   - What similarities and differences are there between this audience and the audience of your letter in Task 1?
   - What is the purpose of your writing?

2 Use your ideas about the audience and purpose of the letter to respond to these questions:
   - How formal will your letter need to be?
   - What techniques for writing to argue do you want to include in your letter?
   - What planning format will best help you to plan your letter?

Composing

Using different text types

1 **Think about the effect on the reader.** As you write, check at the end of each paragraph that you can see what you have done to influence the reader. Have you used a range of ways of presenting your arguments?

Choice of vocabulary

2 As you write, think about the additional words and phrases you can **add** to explain your ideas. For instance, if you add an abstract noun, could you also use an adjective to extend it into a noun phrase?

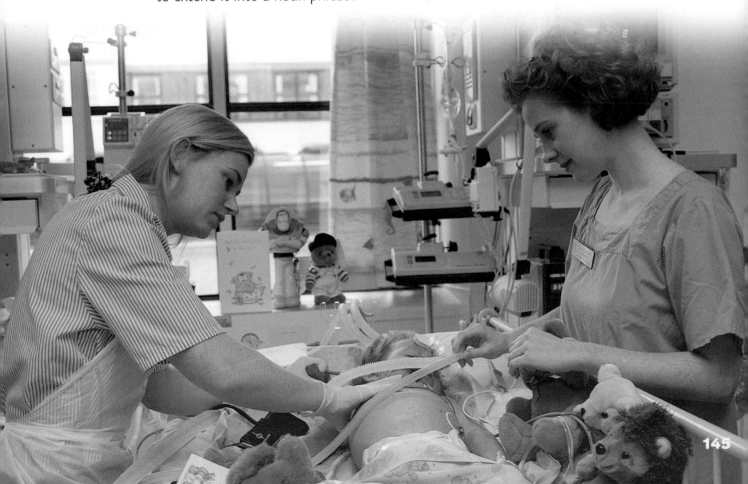

▶ Reviewing

1 You are now going to review your writing with a partner.

   a Read your letter aloud to your partner. As they listen they should make a note of any words or phrases that don't fit the tone you are trying to create. Work together to make **changes** to these to help you maintain a consistent tone.

   b When you have both read your work aloud, discuss the techniques you have used to appeal directly to the audience. Write a short statement at the end of your partner's work summarising what they have done to appeal to the reader. Try to answer the following questions in your statement:

- Is this arguing a case, or is it just telling me about the person?
- Is this formal enough?
- What passages from their writing really interested me?

   c Now read what your partner has written about your letter. Look back at the table in the pre-writing activity on page 137. Which features of writing to argue do you now feel more confident about using? Pick out two techniques you will need to work on in your next piece of argumentative writing.

Imagine, explore, entertain

Successful writers are able to use a range of techniques, structures and styles in order to interest the reader. Often they draw on their knowledge about a wide variety of features in order to achieve their purposes. For example, when presenting an argument a writer could use persuasive techniques to make their argument more powerful. In this unit you will look at writing that aims to imagine and to entertain, but which also uses some of the features of writing to inform and to describe. You will explore how these features can be successfully blended together in a single text and how using different types of sentences can help you to create a tone appropriate for the purpose and audience.

Writing strategies

- see the whole text
- stick to the objectives
- choose how to plan

- use writers' techniques
- changing
- rehearse sentences in your head

Pre-writing: see the whole text

Your work in this unit will explore how texts written to achieve different purposes can contain some of the same features. The Internet site *Great Buildings of Britain* catalogues the important buildings of Britain, such as palaces, museums, theatres and other impressive places, and encourages tourists to visit them. Here is an example entry from the website:

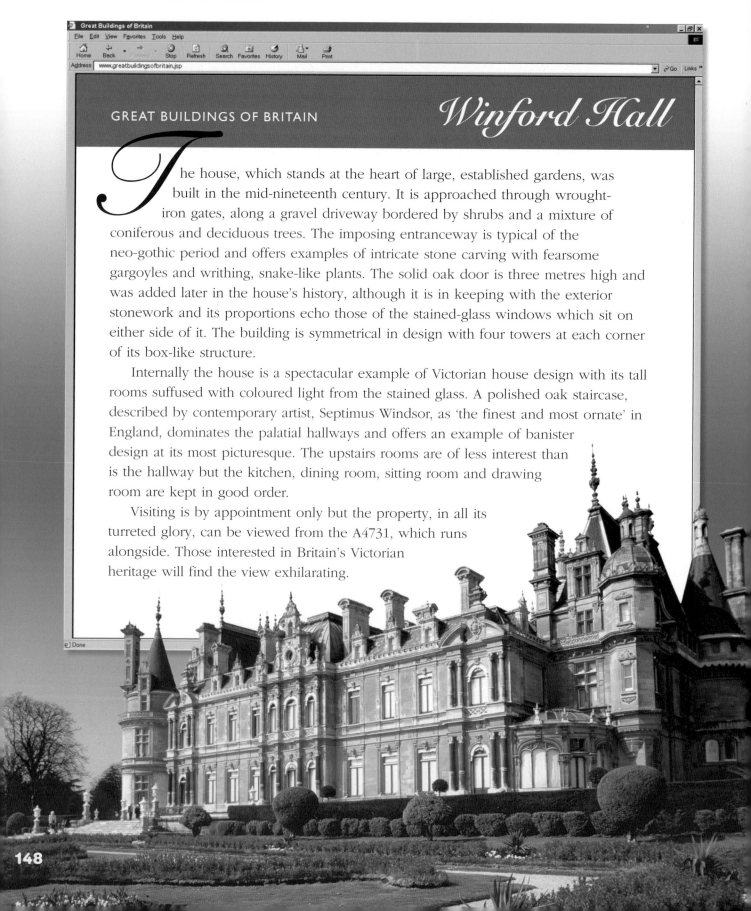

GREAT BUILDINGS OF BRITAIN

Winford Hall

The house, which stands at the heart of large, established gardens, was built in the mid-nineteenth century. It is approached through wrought-iron gates, along a gravel driveway bordered by shrubs and a mixture of coniferous and deciduous trees. The imposing entranceway is typical of the neo-gothic period and offers examples of intricate stone carving with fearsome gargoyles and writhing, snake-like plants. The solid oak door is three metres high and was added later in the house's history, although it is in keeping with the exterior stonework and its proportions echo those of the stained-glass windows which sit on either side of it. The building is symmetrical in design with four towers at each corner of its box-like structure.

Internally the house is a spectacular example of Victorian house design with its tall rooms suffused with coloured light from the stained glass. A polished oak staircase, described by contemporary artist, Septimus Windsor, as 'the finest and most ornate' in England, dominates the palatial hallways and offers an example of banister design at its most picturesque. The upstairs rooms are of less interest than is the hallway but the kitchen, dining room, sitting room and drawing room are kept in good order.

Visiting is by appointment only but the property, in all its turreted glory, can be viewed from the A4731, which runs alongside. Those interested in Britain's Victorian heritage will find the view exhilarating.

1   Working in a small group, complete the following PASS checklist for the text opposite, picking out the features in the text that make the website entry appropriate for its purpose and audience.

- Purpose – to inform the reader about the building and to describe the elements that make it an impressive building that is worth visiting.

- Audience – who is the text aimed at and what does this mean for the content and language used?

- Structure – how is the text organised and how long is it?

- Style – what techniques have been used to fit the purpose and audience?

Great buildings!

You are a writer for the Internet site *Great Buildings of Britain*. Entries on the website normally give information about interesting and impressive buildings, but each year on April Fool's Day a spoof entry about a building of very little interest is published. A spoof is an amusing copy of a more serious piece of writing, which imitates the structure and style of the original to create a humorous effect. Last year's spoof entry was about a public toilet, and began:

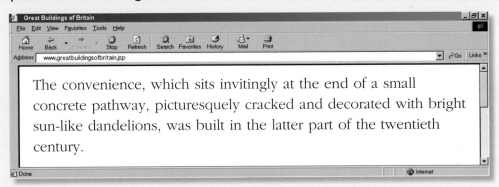

The convenience, which sits invitingly at the end of a small concrete pathway, picturesquely cracked and decorated with bright sun-like dandelions, was built in the latter part of the twentieth century.

You have been asked to write this year's April Fool's Day entry. Imagine that you are trying to encourage people to visit a very ordinary building, such as a garden shed, a bus stop or your own home.

Write an entertaining spoof entry for the website *Great Buildings of Britain*.

Interesting texts

1   In this task you are being asked to write an entry for the website from which you studied an entry in the pre-writing task. However, the purpose of the spoof entry is not the same as that of the other entries on the website. You will need to have a very clear idea of what is being asked of you and then **stick to the objectives**.

   a   Working with a partner, decide what it is you need to do to complete this task and create a PASS checklist for the spoof catalogue entry.

   b   How does this checklist differ from the one that you made in the pre-writing task? In what ways are the two checklists the same? With your partner, discuss how the similarities in the techniques used in the two texts will increase the effectiveness of the spoof entry.

2 Re-read the catalogue entry about the Victorian house on page 148 and answer the questions below to help you identify the features that help to make this text suitable for its purpose and audience.

- Is the entry written in the past tense or the present tense?
- In what order is information presented, for example, is it chronological?
- What sort of connectives are used in the text?
- Is the language used personal or impersonal?
- Does the author use the active or the passive voice?

Think about which of these you will also need to use in your spoof catalogue entry.

Studying a spoof entry

This is last year's April Fool's Day entry from the website *Great Buildings of Britain*.

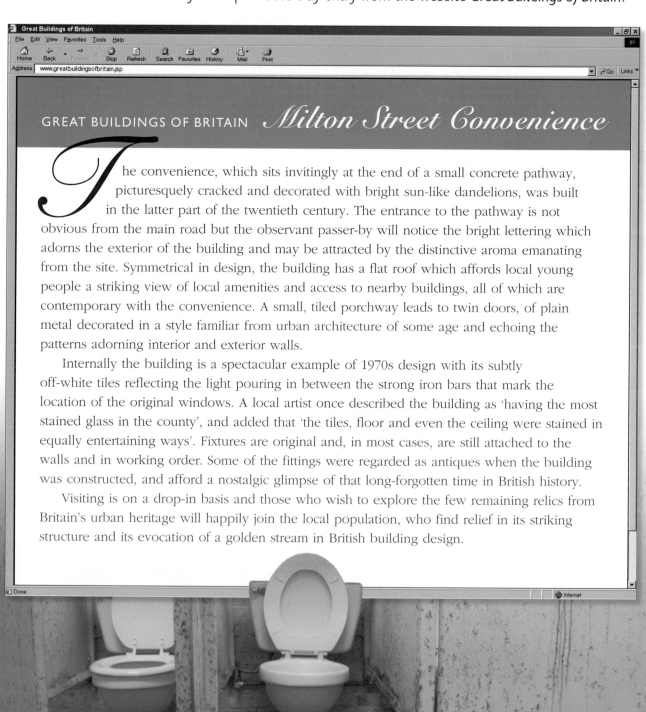

Interesting texts

1   Using the PASS headings, analyse how successful you think this is as a spoof entry for the website. Make notes under each of the PASS headings and discuss the following questions with your partner.

   - Is the entry believable?
   - Does it fit the pattern of more serious entries?
   - What clues are there that it might not be serious?
   - How successful do you think it would be in entertaining its target audience? Why?

Using different types of sentences

Look at both the entry about the Victorian house on page 148 and the spoof entry opposite.

2   On a scale of 1 to 10 in terms of formality (with 10 being very formal and 1 very informal), where would you place these entries? Pick out examples of the following from each entry and comment on the effect they have on the formality of the piece:

   - the use of complex sentences
   - the use of passive sentences
   - the type of vocabulary used.

   Pick out any other techniques that you think are important and contribute to the formality of the text.

3   **a**   How vivid are the descriptions? List the ways in which the writer tries to build a picture for the reader.

   b   Discuss with your partner how the spoof entry balances entertaining the reader with providing a vivid description.

Planning to write

Interesting texts

1   Working with a partner, discuss the different ordinary places you could choose to write about and then select one. Remind yourself to **stick to the objectives** you set out in your PASS checklist for this task. Note down any other ideas you now have about the language, content and structure of the spoof entry you are going to write.

2   You now need to think about the structure of your entry. **Choose how to plan** by selecting an appropriate planning format and organise the ideas from your PASS checklist into sections. As this entry will be included on the *Great Buildings of Britain* website you will need to follow the structure of the other two entries you have read.

Composing

Using different types of sentences

1 Even though you are writing the spoof entry to imagine, explore and entertain, you also have to describe the place you are writing about effectively. This will help to ensure that it meets the expectations of the audience for an entry on the website.

   a Look at the list of **writers' techniques** below. Which do you think will be the most important to use when writing your entry? Rank them in order of importance when communicating a vivid image to the reader:

   - appealing to the senses
   - using a range of punctuation accurately
   - selecting significant details on which to focus
   - using quotations (e.g. from previous visitors) or references (e.g. to other guidebooks)
   - using similes
   - varying sentences
   - using figurative language
   - using contrasts
   - using expanded noun phrases.

   b Write the first draft of your entry. Make sure that you **use the writers' techniques** that you identified as the most important for creating a vivid description of the place you are writing about. Remember that you also need to ensure that you create an entertaining entry for the reader.

Improving

Using different types of sentences

1 Re-read your completed draft. Evaluate how successful you have been in **sticking to the objectives** set out in your PASS checklist. **Change** any sentences or vocabulary that you think are too informal. Check that you have created a vivid and entertaining description and make any changes that you think will help you to improve this.

2 Remember, you have a limited amount of space in a catalogue entry. Read through the sentences you have written. Are there any ways you could reduce the number of words used while still keeping the detail and meaning?

▶ Reviewing

1 Swap your piece of writing with a partner and ask them to identify the features that you have used. How effective will your spoof catalogue entry be at entertaining the reader and matching their expectations for an entry on this website? Discuss how successfully you have **stuck to the objectives** in your PASS checklist and what you would like to improve next time.

SW Task 2 — A new perspective

You are a presenter on a radio travel programme famous for creating clear and vivid pictures of places using language alone. For a special children's edition of the programme which is going to be broadcast at Christmas you have been asked to describe a travel location with a difference – a fairy-tale location such as the seven dwarves' cottage from *Snow White* or the giant's castle from *Jack and the Beanstalk*.

Write the script for the children's edition of the radio programme describing the fairy-tale location in an entertaining way.

Planning to write

Interesting texts

1   Create a PASS checklist to help you **stick to the objectives**:

   • Purpose – what does this text have to do?
   • Audience – who is the text aimed at and what does this mean for the content and the language you will use?
   • Structure – how should the text be organised and how long should it be?
   • Style – what techniques will you have to use in order to meet the demands of the task?

   Remember to think about how a script for a radio programme differs from a website entry and consider the level of formality required. What will you need to think about when writing for a scripted performance on radio?

2   Decide on a fairy story you know well (or could easily research) to help you choose the location you will describe. What are the key features of this location?

3   **Choose how to plan** and note down the key features of the location. **Add** some details from the fairy story to help you include some humorous touches, for example 'this is the very room where Goldilocks ate Baby Bear's bowl of porridge'.

Using different types of sentences

4   Return to the list of **writers' techniques** opposite. Which of these techniques do you think should be prioritised here? Add notes on how to use these to your plan.

Composing

Using different types of sentences

1   As you write, **rehearse sentences in your head**. Remember, this is the script for a radio programme so you should be hearing it and thinking about how it sounds. Think about the way you will **stick to the objectives** in your PASS checklist.

Improving

Using different types of sentences

1   **a**   Swap your completed draft with a partner who should read yours aloud to you. How does it sound? Read your partner's writing aloud to them, sticking strictly to the punctuation. Were you able to read it fluently?

　　b   Discuss the **changes** you could make to improve your writing and redraft the script.

▶ Reviewing

1   You will now record your script for broadcast. Remember to follow your script exactly when recording. Working in a group of four, listen back to the recording and make notes on how well you have **stuck to the objectives** in your checklist that you were pursuing.